"Dr. Olford has done it again! . . . biblical exposition for preachers and a model of contagious Christian living for the people of God. A must read!"

—Leroy R. Armstrong Jr., Senior Pastor
Greater Good Hope Baptist Church, Louisville, Kentucky

"In a day of uncertainty, worldwide upheaval, and instability, Stephen Olford hits the target with hope and surety. . . . The twenty-first century challenges us with the threat of incredible change and possible worldwide chaos. However, deep assurance and peace come to the person who chooses to obey the One who created this world. Throughout his book, Dr. Olford encourages us to be all we can and to show the world that Christ really does make a difference in our lives."

—Wayde I. Goodall, National Coordinator,
Ministerial Enrichment
The Assemblies of God

"Vintage Stephen Olford! With clarity, accuracy, and compelling insights, my mentor and friend calls us to embrace authentic Christianity. The message of this book will stimulate your mind and refresh your soul."

—Crawford W. Loritts Jr., Associate U.S. Director
Campus Crusade for Christ

Despite the unparalleled advances in the fields of technology and other scientific endeavors, our day is plagued by a great deal of fuzzy thinking, especially in the disciplines of philosophy, morality, and religion. Christianity has been victimized by this scourge, not only from those without but also from many within the professed church. The question, "What is the Christian message?" would evoke a confusing cluster of replies, yet it is capable of being reduced to a common denominator: Do good! In a word, the effect of the Christian message is mistaken for the message itself.

—From the Introduction

THE
CHRISTIAN
MESSAGE
FOR
CONTEMPORARY
LIFE

The Gospel's Power to Change Lives

STEPHEN F. OLFORD

PUBLICATIONS

Grand Rapids, MI 49501

Published by Kregel Publications, a division of Kregel, Inc., P.O. Box 2607, Grand Rapids, MI 49501. Kregel Publications provides trusted, biblical publications for Christian growth and service. Your comments and suggestions are valued.

For more information about Kregel Publications, visit our web site at www.kregel.com.

Cover design: Frank Gutbrod
Book design: Nicholas G. Richardson

Library of Congress Cataloging-in-Publication Data
Olford, Stephen F.
   The Christian message for contemporary life: the gospel's power to change lives / Stephen F. Olford.
      p.   cm.
      1. Bible. N.T. 1 Corinthians—Commentaries. I. Title.
BS2675.3.045   1999   227'.2077—dc21   99-18856
                                             CIP
ISBN 0-8254-3361-4

Printed in the United States of America

1 2 3 4 5 / 03 02 01 00 99

To Preachers of the Gospel

The chapters in this book are messages delivered to audiences around the world and in churches I have served. In the "flow" of such preaching, many quotes, concepts, and illustrations were brought to mind without specific documentation. I therefore acknowledge all sources of such material—heard or read—from the "gifts of men" (Eph. 4:8) with which our risen Lord has enriched the church.

CONTENTS

FOREWORD

With clear insight infused throughout his alliterative style, Stephen Olford has given us a significant and succinct presentation of the first three chapters of 1 Corinthians. Although he has dedicated the work to preachers of the gospel of Jesus Christ, it contains a contemporary message for the pastor and layperson alike. Dr. Olford's exposition of the Word of God is enlightening and challenging as well as a source of spiritual truth.

Here is biblical exposition at its best. The overarching theme throughout the presentation is the commission of our Lord recorded in Acts 1:8: "You shall receive power when the Holy Spirit has come upon you; and you shall be witnesses to Me in Jerusalem, and in all Judea and Samaria, and to the end of the earth." In the preface of this excellent work, Olford makes it clear that Christ's commission applies to all God's people. Every believer must be involved in lifting up Jesus Christ to a very needy world.

Moreover, we live in a day with radio, television, computers, and astonishing advancements in transportation and literacy, which make the fulfilling of the commission more of a possibility than perhaps at any time in the history of the church. The challenge is there, and God expects His people to respond.

Stephen Olford makes very clear that in the entirety of Christian commitment, Jesus Christ, the Savior of the world, is at the heart. The church at Corinth missed this principle, and so Paul wrote to correct the fundamental error. If ever the church is to fulfill its commission, it will be because Jesus Christ is exalted for who He is—for *all* He is—and because this message is passionately presented to a struggling society. Olford's study makes for fascinating reading. Stephen has done a superb job, filling the book with excellent and captivating illustrations and quotes, and with Christ always at the core it is the kind of a book that one finds hard to put down. The key to its gripping message revolves around the fact that Christ is lifted up. Furthermore, the author puts the church in its proper place and perspective. Considering the current criticism of the church and the diminution of the importance of the church in the minds of many, Stephen gives us a timely message. As he expresses it, all true believers are members of the church and should affiliate themselves with a local manifestation of Christ's body.

Every page rings with a passion to present Jesus Christ from the standpoint of a Spirit-filled, Spirit-guided, Christ-exalting stance. Throughout the entire book, commitment to Jesus Christ is stressed. This exhortation lays the foundation for effective communication of the message to contemporary society. As Count Zinzendorf declared concerning his passion for Christ, "I have only one passion, it is He, only He." The great reformer Martin Luther exemplified this spirit in his life and ministry also. Olford quotes Luther's well-known statement: "I preach as though Christ was crucified yesterday, rose again from the dead today, and is coming back to earth tomorrow." Jesus stands as the supreme passion of the communicator. This Christ-centered stance constantly surfaces in all that Olford's pungent biblical expositions set forth.

When one reads this book carefully, with a heart open to the moving of the Holy Spirit in and through the scriptural truths presented, the results will be deeply and profoundly significant:

• Christ will be exalted.
• The gospel will be made clear.
• The church will be put in proper perspective.
• Encouragement and wisdom for witnessing will be grasped.
• Godliness and spiritual growth will be developed.

Any work that can achieve these stellar accomplishments is well worth one's full and serious reading; Stephen Olford meets these objectives in his book. I most heartily commend it to any true Christian seeker who wants to communicate the message of Christ in today's world.

DR. LEWIS A. DRUMMOND
Billy Graham Professor of Evangelism
and Church Growth
Beeson Divinity School, Birmingham, Alabama

PREFACE

In his little book *Man Alive*,[1] Michael Green quotes Lord Eccles who scolds church leaders today for the unintelligibility and irrelevance of so much theological writing. His words of criticism need to be weighed and heeded when he says, "The laity, although better informed on almost everything else, have never been so ignorant about the groundplan of the New Testament." And then addressing the clergy he adds, "This is partly your fault because you have concentrated your scholarships in fields too narrow to be widely interesting; will you now turn your attention to the gospel as a whole? to its relevance as a whole to the age in which we live?" Michael Green has taken Lord Eccles seriously and has written an excellent treatment of the resurrection of our Lord Jesus Christ, showing its contemporary relevance, challenge, and power to change men's lives. What is even more important is that he has couched this central fact of our Christian faith in terms that the layman can understand.

Even before I read *Man Alive* I was burdened in a similar fashion for young Christians who find it so difficult to appreciate and communicate the Christian message to their contemporaries, so I set about preparing a series of messages that I first delivered at a crusade. My audience was mainly young people, so I spoke accordingly, and I trust, appropriately. The response of these youthful listeners was so overwhelmingly positive that I was asked to share these studies in printed form. I was hesitant to comply with the condition that the material be published as I had preached it. This I had never done before, since to do so would violate my literary style! However, with some deletions of irrelevant asides and redundant words, I agreed to release the manuscript. It is my sincere prayer that the Holy Spirit will graciously use the preaching format, with its fire and challenge, to bless readers as it did those who heard the message.

The outlines that introduce each chapter are included to aid ministers and Christian workers in tracing the expository treatment of the first three chapters of 1 Corinthians. It follows, therefore, that to derive the greatest benefit from these studies, it would be well to read and reread the verses that constitute the text.

Nearly two thousand years ago our risen Savior said, "Go into all the world and preach the gospel to every creature" (Mark 16:15). Dr. Alexander Maclaren called this "the divine audacity of Christianity." A study of the commission, as it appears in other parts of the New Testament, makes it manifestly clear that the Lord Jesus meant literally *all* the world. He meant every country of the world, for He said, "You shall receive power when the Holy Spirit has come upon you; and you shall be witnesses to Me in Jerusalem, and in all Judea and Samaria, and to the end of the earth" (Acts 1:8). No country is to be left out.

Jesus meant every culture of the world. "Go therefore and make disciples of all the nations, baptizing them in the name of the Father and of the Son and of the Holy Spirit, teaching them to observe all things that I have commanded you; and lo, I am with you always, even to the end of the age" (Matt. 28:19–20). We are living in a day of emerging nations. Never before in the history of the world has such emphasis been placed on the dignity, unity, and sovereignty of individual nations. Because great importance is also attached to the culture of these nations, Christianity is often rejected, since it is associated with Western culture. But notwithstanding these difficulties, the commission is to go to every nation.

And our Master meant every creature of the world. "Go into all the world and preach the gospel to every creature" (Mark 16:15). God is no respecter of persons, and therefore man, whatever his color, creed, or class, must be reached with this glorious message of full salvation.

When the Lord Jesus uttered these words the world was not accessible to the preacher and missionary as it is today, but we have no excuse now. Some years ago the president of the Royal Geographical Society (U.K.) chose a startling phrase to describe the modern world. He said, "Time and distance have now been annihilated by modern inventions and have caused *a shrinkage of the globe*." We have radio, television, computers, the Internet, and astonishing advances in literacy and available literature. Having said all this, however, we must hang our heads in shame when we realize that there are millions of people who have never heard the gospel of our Lord Jesus Christ, and that every day of every year hundreds of thousands die without hope of eternal life. How urgent and solemn, then, is our task to carry the Christian message to contemporary people! May God give us the grace to catch the vision, feel the passion, and serve the mission of our commissioning Lord.

STEPHEN F. OLFORD

ACKNOWLEDGMENTS

The author gratefully acknowledges the efforts of Jennifer Balmer, my projects assistant, in typing and preparing this manuscript.

I must thank my dear friend and colleague Dr. Lewis Drummond, Billy Graham Professor of Evangelism and Church Growth at Beeson Divinity School in Birmingham, Alabama, for writing the foreword. As always, he is lucid, learned, and lovable! Thank you, dear brother!

INTRODUCTION

Despite the unparalleled advances in the fields of technology and other scientific endeavors, our day is plagued by a great deal of fuzzy thinking, especially in the disciplines of philosophy, morality, and religion. Christianity has been victimized by this scourge, not only from those without but also from many within the professed church. The question, "What is the Christian message?" would evoke a confusing cluster of replies, yet it is capable of being reduced to a common denominator: Do good! In a word, the effect of the Christian message is mistaken for the message itself.

Postmodernism has influenced many pastors in our land to preach what people want to hear. (This was true in Paul's day; see 2 Tim. 4:1–4). Postmodernists tell us to quit preaching sin and repentance. People don't want to hear anything negative. We need to give them a positive "feeling."

Of course, repentance hurts; but people need to hear the demands of God's holy law. This is particularly true in this age of moral relativism. We need to be convicted of sin in order to turn in faith to God's forgiveness in Jesus Christ.

Jesus as Savior and Lord is the Christian message, and in no place in Scripture is this more clearly delineated than in 1 Corinthians 1:9–3:4. Significantly, the apostle finds himself facing a schismatic situation in the Corinthian church.

In dealing with this problem, he does not merely reprove it, but corrects it by presenting only the Christian message, which promises and promotes unity in Christ. When we grasp the wonder of the message, discrimination or division over the messengers or any other lesser consideration is ruled out.

In the chapters before us, I have sought to follow the keen reasoning of the apostle Paul in order to show the relevancy of the Christian message for our generation. More than ever people need a gospel that brings the wisdom and the power of God to meet their intellectual and moral concerns. They need a gospel that reaches the foolish, the feeble, and the fallen, for that is as much the state of a twentieth-century person as of a first-century person. There is no such gospel, save that of "Jesus Christ, and Him crucified." This is the apostolic emphasis, and this is the sword-thrust of this book.

These studies are published essentially as they were delivered, so that the preaching style, warm and pointed, comes through. It is my prayer that you will be moved by the reading, as so many were by the hearing, of these expository messages.

1 Corinthians 1:9-17

I. Division Paralyzes the Fellowship of the Church in Its Witness to the World (v. 10)
   A. Division in the Church Degrades the Ministry of the Word of God (v. 10)
   B. Division in the Church Disrupts the Unity of the Spirit of God (v. 10)
II. Division Publicizes the Membership of the Church in Its Witness to the World (v. 11)
   A. Division Adversely Publicizes the Name of the Church (v. 11)
   B. Division Adversely Publicizes the Fame of the Church (v. 11)
III. Division Polarizes the Leadership of the Church in Its Witness to the World (v. 12)
   A. Devotion to Men Rather than the Master (v. 12)
      1. There Were Those Who Said They Belonged to Paul
      2. There Were Those Who Said They Belonged to Apollos
      3. There Were Those Who Said They Belonged to Cephas
      4. There Were Those Who Said They Belonged to Christ
   B. Attention to Messengers Rather than the Message (vv. 13–17)

Chapter ONE

THE CONTRADICTION
OF THE CHRISTIAN MESSAGE

I have elected to deal with "The Christian Message for Contemporary Life" because of the new evangelical interest that is emerging in our country and in lands overseas at this present time. Of course many things still concern us and drive us to our knees, but it is evident that evangelists who have been on the sidelines for some time are finding extended and exciting opportunities for crusades and other gospel activities. Young people, particularly, are giving a significant lead with their singing, witnessing, and marching for Christ! The Spirit of God has been poured out in an unusual manner on some of our churches in the U.S.A. and elsewhere. Individuals have come into a fresh experience of what it means to be anointed with the Holy Spirit and to speak and serve with power from on high.

With this in mind, I invite you to peruse the first chapters of 1 Corinthians. We shall look first at 1 Corinthians 1:9–17.

God is faithful, by whom you were called into the fellowship of His Son, Jesus Christ our Lord. Now I plead with you, brethren, by the name of our Lord

Jesus Christ, that you all speak the same thing, and that there be no divisions among you, but that you be perfectly joined together in the same mind and in the same judgment. For it has been declared to me concerning you, my brethren, by those of Chloe's household, that there are contentions among you. Now I say this, that each of you says, "I am of Paul," or "I am of Apollos," or "I am of Cephas," or "I am of Christ." Is Christ divided? Was Paul crucified for you? Or were you baptized in the name of Paul? I thank God that I baptized none of you except Crispus and Gaius, lest anyone should say that I had baptized in my own name.

Yes, I also baptized the household of Stephanas. Besides, I do not know whether I baptized any other. For Christ did not send me to baptize, but to preach the gospel, not with wisdom of words, lest the cross of Christ should be made of no effect.

Under our main theme, "The Christian Message for Contemporary Life," we shall consider in order "The Contradiction of the Christian Message," "The Character of the Christian Message," "The Community of the Christian Message," "The Communication of the Christian Message," "The Comprehension of the Christian Message," and "The Challenge of the Christian Message."

Our immediate concern, then, is "The Contradiction of the Christian Message" (1 Cor. 1:9–17). To examine this portion of the New Testament is to be impressed not only with the annunciation of God's grace but also with the evaluation of human need. Before he deals with these cardinal doctrines, the apostle addresses the problem that had weakened the witness of the Corinthian church and, indeed, has weakened the church of Jesus Christ at every stage of her history—the problem of *division*. Our Savior prayed against this when He faced the death of the cross, looked on to the day of Pentecost, and anticipated the discipling of the nations. Addressing His Father He prayed, "[Make my disciples] one, as You . . . are in Me, and I in You; that they also may be one in Us, *that the world may believe that You sent Me*" (John 17:21).

The apostle had the same burden on his heart when he wrote to the church at Philippi. Mark well his words, "Only let your conduct be worthy of the gospel of Christ . . . that you stand fast in one spirit, with one mind striving together for the faith of the gospel" (Phil. 1:27). His point is that nothing contradicts our Christian message like division in the church. How can we preach the message of reconciliation when Christians cannot forgive one another? How can we proclaim the gospel of peace when church members are at one another's throats? So in the verses before us Paul confronts this issue head-on. In verse 9 he starts with the affirmation that "God is faithful, by whom [all Christians are] called into the fellowship of His Son, Jesus Christ our Lord." And then, without a break, he continues, "Now I plead with you, brethren, by the name of our Lord Jesus Christ, that you all speak the same thing, and that there be no divisions among you, but that you be perfectly joined together in the same mind and in the same judgment" (v. 10). We cannot compare verses 9 and 10 with any measure of perceptiveness without concluding that the supreme contradiction of the Christian message is division in the church. Observe carefully how Paul supports this deduction.

First, *division paralyzes the fellowship of the church in its witness to the world.* "Now I plead with you, brethren, by the name of our Lord Jesus Christ, that you all speak the same thing, and that there be no divisions among you, but that you be perfectly joined together in the same mind and in the same judgment" (v. 10). Christian fellowship, as we all know, is based on two fundamental prerequisites for a local church: first, the ministry of the Word of God, and second, the unity of the Spirit of God. You will remember that after the day of Pentecost the early disciples "continued steadfastly in the apostles' doctrine and fellowship" (Acts 2:42). Let us recognize that there can be no true fellowship without a doctrinal basis. When writing to the Philippians, Paul speaks of this fellowship, this *koinonia,* as the "fellowship of the Spirit" (2:1). So we see that it is only through the truth of God that we are brought to the reconciling death of Christ, and it is only through the Spirit of God that we are brought to the unifying life of Christ. Wonderful as all this is, nothing is more calculated to paralyze the fellowship of the church in its witness to the world than division, for division strikes at the heart of these fundamental prerequisites.

Division in the church degrades the ministry of the Word of God. "I plead with you, brethren, by the name of our Lord Jesus Christ, that you *all speak the same thing.*" Division paralyzes the fellowship of the church because there is no unity of witness in what we say; and that was true at Corinth. The strength of any testimony is that everyone says *the same thing.* In his appeal to the Corinthian church for a united front, Paul employs an expression that was used in political circles for "mutual agreement" or "perfect agreement." He was not suggesting uniformity of speech. There are many ways of saying the same thing. Styles of presentation may and do differ, but truth is unchanging and unchangeable. There is a unity of testimony that must be the result of the acceptance and declaration of the truth of God. How well history illustrates this again and again! The impact of the church of Jesus Christ has been considerable when the church has said the same thing. Lloyd George, that great politician and one-time prime minister of Great Britain, is reputed to have said that "whenever there was a moral question to settle, once the bells of the church rang in unison the battle was over." When Christians say the same thing there is unity of strength, and the world outside believes. It is what our Savior prayed for when He expressed, "[Make them] one, as You, Father, are in Me, and I in You; that they also may be one in Us, *that the world may believe that You sent Me*" (John 17:21). So Paul strongly appeals to the Corinthians to speak the same thing.

Division in the church not only degrades the ministry of the Word of God but disrupts the unity of the Spirit of God. "I plead with you, brethren, by the name of our Lord Jesus Christ . . . that you be perfectly joined together in the same mind and in the same judgment" (v. 10). There is an essential unity that nothing can ever harm or destroy. As John Stott has put it, "Our unity in Christ is essentially as strong as the unity between the Father and the Son and the Holy Spirit." Nothing can divide us from the love of God that is in Christ Jesus our Lord (Rom. 8:38–39). There is a fundamental unity that nothing can change. On the other hand, there is an experimental unity that can be interrupted by division. There is a rift that can come into the personal fellowship of your church, your group, even your family, and that is what Paul is speaking about here. He is saddened by the fact that the seamless robe of unity has been torn within the Christian community. The word he selects to describe this condition is the one from which we derive our term *schism*. He says there is a schism, a rent, in the garment. William Barclay remarks, "The Christian Church was in danger of becoming as unsightly as a torn garment."[1] And Paul admonishes, "I plead with you, brethren . . . that you be perfectly joined together in the same mind and in the same judgment" (v. 10). The phrase, "perfectly joined together," conveys a beautiful concept. It is used in the Gospels of "mending nets." It is used in the First Epistle of Paul to the Thessalonians for supplying a lack (3:10). Quite clearly reparation was desperately needed in the Corinthian church; thus the apostle pleads for it in no uncertain language. He calls for a unity of mind, a harmony of judgment. Only such a return to the unity of the Word of God, only such a return to the unity of the Spirit of God could bring about a united front and a gospel for the times in which Paul lived. What was true then is true today.

In 1747 there arose differences and disunity among Moravian brethren who belonged to a group of local churches whose influence and missionary effort were widespread. Count Zinzendorf, with representative elders, arranged to hold a conference at which the differing views on the subject of their controversy might be aired and discussed amicably. The leaders came, some from long distances, to the place where the conference was to be held. Arriving on the appointed day, each prepared to contest the view he supported, confident that it would receive the acceptance of the majority. In his wisdom, Zinzendorf proposed that they should spend some time in the Word and in prayer. The book chosen for study was the First Epistle of John, and for several days they examined the teaching of this letter, learning that one of its main lessons was "love for all the brethren." They agreed that on the first day of the week, like the disciples in the early church, they should come together to break bread, and so be reminded that they, being many, were "one Body." The reading and studying of God's Word and the fellowship at the Lord's Supper had a very salutary effect on all. Indeed, the result was such that when they commenced on Monday morning to examine the matters on which they differed, they discovered that their disputes had been settled as each had bowed to the Word of God. Oh, that we might learn to settle our disagreements and divisions in a similar fashion!

But there is another aspect to this division. Division

paralyzes the fellowship of the church, to be sure, but more than that, *division publicizes the membership of the church in its witness to the world*. "For it has been declared to me concerning you, my brethren, by those of Chloe's household, that there are contentions among you" (v. 11). Whether we like to admit it or not, there is no such thing as an isolated or insulated local church. Whatever happens inside becomes known outside. In terms of spreading the gospel, this is one of the main functions of the local church; unfortunately, the same thing holds true when it comes to things we do not want to expose or disclose. So we find that division publicizes the membership of the local church in a twofold manner.

Division adversely publicizes the *name* of the church: "For it has been declared to me concerning you, my brethren, by those of Chloe's household" (v. 11). The identity of Chloe is not fully revealed to us, but with fair accuracy we can state that this wealthy lady, with her household, was known throughout the membership. And some of the servants of her household, traveling between Ephesus and Corinth, had brought the account of the divided state of the church to the attention of the apostle. So Paul takes pains to assert that what he had heard was not gossip or rumor. The Greek he employs signifies that his informant had disclosed with accuracy the sad situation. To confirm the report, Paul actually names Chloe and her household. If the apostle had learned of "the contentions" in far off Ephesus, how about the rest of the church at Corinth, the believers in the surrounding environs, and the pagan world looking on?

Jesus taught His disciples that they were to be known by their love one towards another (John 13:34–35). There were first-century Christians who loved one another in such a manner that the outside world stood back and said, "See how these Christians love one another." Alas, so many in the world stand back today as they look at our local churches, and say, "See how these Christians fight one another!" There can be no worse publicity for the membership of any church than news of division.

For many years it has been my privilege to conduct city-wide crusades throughout the British Isles, the United States of America, and Canada. I can testify that when churches have united for Christian witness, the spiritual impact has been tremendous: souls have been saved, saints have been edified, and times of refreshment have been experienced from the presence of the Lord. On the other hand, when denominational differences or personal prejudices have characterized such efforts, the going has been hard, the results have been negligible, and the world has questioned the reality and relevance of the Christian message. More likely than not, the press has carried adverse publicity.

But not only does division adversely publicize the name of the church, it also adversely publicizes the *fame* of the church. Look at verse 11 carefully. "For it has been declared to me . . . that there are *contentions* among you." The word "contention" is one that the apostle Paul uses in Galatians 5:20 to condemn an ugly manifestation of the flesh. It denotes wrangling as opposed to orderly discussion and leads to aroused feelings and shameful quarrels. Tragically, the Corinthian church was famous for this.

There is a church in the U.S.A. that was headlined in local and national papers for "splits" and "schisms." My heart bled as I read the account, for I happen to know the history of that church. Many missionaries have been sent out from that fellowship, but now it is divided down the middle. The rival group has started another church while the rest of the members are floundering, trying to find themselves. The church has become famous, but *adversely* famous.

If Christians only knew it, this is exactly what Satan is out to do in every local church. His mission is to disrupt, divide, and destroy the Christian community. We join hands with the devil when we allow perverse activity to scandalize the membership. Whatever good a local church or congregation may do in the neighborhood by way of witnessing for Christ, preaching the gospel, or visiting the homes is eclipsed when there are quarrels, backbitings, and contentions. If Christians would only recognize the irreparable damage done by division, they would do everything in their power to maintain "the unity of the Spirit in the bond of peace" (Eph. 4:3). Essentially we are one, because we are linked to the Father and the Son and the Holy Spirit, but it is our task to translate that unity into visibility by covering one another's failings with fervent love so that the world never gets to know of our petty differences (1 Peter 4:8).

Jonathan Goforth, in his book *By My Spirit,* writes of a revival in Korea in 1904 that swept thousands into the kingdom. It started, however, when he, as a senior missionary, went to a fellow worker and apologized for harbored misunderstandings. As the two hearts were melted before God, the Holy Spirit was poured out as "floods upon dry ground."

We must mark with soberness that division not only paralyzes the fellowship and publicizes the membership of the church but also *polarizes the leadership of the church in its witness to the world.* "Now I say this, that each of you says, 'I am of Paul,' or 'I am of Apollos,' or 'I am of Cephas,' or 'I am of Christ'" (v. 12). There were some outstanding leaders associated with the church at Corinth, and their ministry had been unmistakably owned by God; but through dissension among the members the leadership was polarized in two ways.

First, there was devotion to men rather than the Master—"Now I say this, that each of you says, 'I am of Paul,' or 'I am of Apollos,' or 'I am of Cephas,' or 'I am of Christ'" (v. 12). Division in the church is usually an evidence that eyes have turned away from our blessed Lord Jesus Christ to men. So we find that four parties emerged.

There were those who said they belonged to Paul and constituted the liberalist party. Paul had preached the gospel of liberty. His message was, "Stand fast therefore in the liberty by which Christ has made us free, and do not be entangled again with a yoke of bondage" (Gal. 5:1). It is most likely, therefore, that the members of this group were primarily Gentiles who had attempted to turn Christian liberty into carnal license. This was their excuse to do what they liked.

There were those who said they belonged to Apollos and constituted the philosophical-religious party. Apollos was the product of the famous schools of Alexandria and, therefore, essentially a philosopher at heart. He was master of the intellectual approach, the allegorical presentation, and the rhetorical delivery. As a preacher he was "mighty in the Scriptures" (Acts 18:24) and, consequently, made a strong appeal to the intellectuals of Corinth, with comparisons unfavorable to the apostle Paul.

There were those who said they belonged to Cephas and constituted the legalistic party. Cephas, as you may know, is the Jewish form of the name Peter. This group was made up of Hebrew Christians who maintained that a person must observe the Jewish law. These people regarded Peter as preeminent among the twelve disciples of the Lord Jesus Christ, and therefore, supreme amongst the apostles.

Then there were those who claimed they belonged to Christ and constituted the separatistic party. This was a self-righteous sect who posed as if they were the only true Christians in Corinth. Their real fault was not in saying they belonged to Christ but in acting as if Christ belonged to them alone.

While the parties may have had some theological differences, the main issue on which they were divided was not one of principle but of personality. So unbalanced had they become in their devotion to certain leaders that they dared to assert that they belonged to them. They were guilty of the most damaging personality cult; and sad to say, this is one of the great problems in the Christian world today. Our churches are polarized by factions and followers that are associated with so-called "big names." Because one leader holds a certain position while his opposite number takes a different stance, their respective "disciples" invariably overreact and cause division. As believers, we seem to know so little of the inner strengthening of the Spirit to "*comprehend with all the saints* what is the width and length and depth and height . . . [of] the love of Christ" (Eph. 3:18–19).

Therefore, we find Paul in the following verse asking with evident indignation: "Is Christ divided? Was Paul crucified for you? Or were you baptized in the name of Paul?" (v. 13). The whole purpose of these penetrating questions was to show the utter absurdity, if not blasphemy, of lowering the Person of the Lord Jesus Christ to the level of human leadership. Paul was underscoring the fact that Christ is Head not only of the total church but also of the local church. Only as this is acknowledged can human leadership be authorized and recognized.

The passage goes on to say that the church was polarized not only by devotion to men rather than the Master but also by attention to messengers rather than the message. Paul says, "I thank God that I baptized none of you except Crispus and Gaius, lest anyone should say that I had baptized in my own name. Yes, I also baptized the household of Stephanas. Besides, I do not know whether I baptized any other. For Christ did not send me to baptize, but to preach the gospel" (vv. 14–17). In their carnality and divisiveness, these Corinthians had become so attracted to the messengers of the gospel that they had forgotten the message of the gospel. They were more impressed with the sacraments than they were with the Scriptures, more involved with the ordinances than with obedience. So Paul states with an obvious sense of relief, "I thank God that I baptized none of you except Crispus and Gaius" (v. 14).

In saying this, the apostle was not belittling baptism. In fact, the people Paul had baptized were very special converts, as a study of their names reveals; but so prone were these Corinthians to give personal allegiance to the one who had baptized them that they had overlooked the importance of the message that Paul had preached. In no sense was Paul seeking to minimize sacred ordinances or style of preaching; his burden was to turn the attention of the Corinthians away from the messengers to the message. The Christ into whom a person is baptized is more important than the ordinance; the message of the gospel is more important than the method of delivery. As John Stott has written:

> All Christian work is fraught with great peril, and none more so than that of the Christian ministry. It is possible to engage in the ministry of the Word and sacraments, to preach and to baptize in such a way as to attach men and women to ourselves instead of to Christ . . . . The Word and sacraments bear witness to Christ. Preaching is the proclamation of Christ crucified. Baptism is baptism into the name of Christ crucified. We must exalt Christ in both, not men; the person who matters is not the one who preaches but the One who is preached; not the one who baptizes but the Christ into whom we are baptized.

So the ultimate remedy for a divided church is a return to the centrality of the Lord Jesus Christ. Paul emphasizes this right throughout the opening paragraphs of this epistle. Underscore the name of the Lord Jesus every time it is mentioned in the first seventeen verses. You will find that in this short paragraph Christ is mentioned fourteen times! The Corinthians had decentralized Christ, and so had divided the church. Paul, therefore, brings them back to the name of the Lord Jesus Christ, the One in whom they believed, the One into whom they had been baptized. Thus for a fellowship that is paralyzed, a membership that is publicized, and a leadership that is polarized, the answer is ever and only Christ in all the glory of His Person and preeminence in the church. God had decreed that this is how it should be if we are to know the fullness of heaven's benediction (Col. 1:18–19).

Let us remember, however, that the local church is made up of individual Christians. The issues that divide the membership are precisely the issues that divide my heart and yours. James convincingly argues this when he asks, "Where do wars and fights come from among you? Do they not come from your desires for pleasure that war in your members?" (4:1). Where there is division in our hearts it is soon reflected in the fellowship, in the membership, and in the leadership. It follows, therefore, that before our witness can become effective to the world outside, we have to become united inside, whether as a church or as individual Christians. This is what the psalmist means when he prays, "Teach me Your way, O LORD; I will walk in Your truth; unite my heart to fear Your name" (Psalm 86:11). The united heart expresses itself in a life that cannot be challenged, and this is what the world is looking for today. This is why the Lord Jesus made such an impact upon His contemporaries. When people heard Him speak they were astonished at His authority. The secret was that His preaching and His practice were united. The unity of His heart was the essence of His authority. No one could question His devotion to God or His compassion towards men. There was no contradiction in His life or in His message.

As we conclude this study, I ask this searching but simple question: Are we religious contradictions, or are we real Christians?

Seldom have I been so challenged as by a missionary couple who had just returned from the mission field. In her report, the young wife told of the severe restrictions on the proclamation of the gospel and the distribution of Christian literature. She explained that even in conversation she was not allowed to discuss Christianity unless directly asked for "a reason of the hope that was in her." Then she added quietly, "In my part of the world, my life must demand a supernatural explanation, or there is no chance to witness, no Christ to offer. My life is my message, and *what I am counts far more than what I say*."

If you and I were placed in similar circumstances would our lives contradict the gospel, or would they commend the gospel? What contribution are you making? What contribution am I making to a world that is watching and waiting for a demonstration of unchallengeable Christianity? Can you and I say, "My life is my message"?

1 Corinthians 1:18-25

Contemporary Revolutions in our World
1. Revolution of a Spiraling Technology
2. Revolution of a Rising Expectation
3. Revolution of an Emerging Generation
4. Revolution of a Changing Culture
5. Revolution of a Declining Religion

I. The Christian Message Is God's Distinctive Revelation to Mankind (v. 18)
   A. The Wisdom of God with the Wisdom of Man (v. 24)
      1. The Wisdom of God (v. 30)
         a) The Revelation of Christ as Our Righteousness (v. 30)
         b) The Revelation of Christ as Our Sanctification (v. 30)
         c) The Revelation of Christ as Our Redemption (v. 30)
      2. The Wisdom of Man (v. 21)
         a) Human Wisdom Is Earthly (v. 21)
         b) Human Wisdom Is Sensual (v. 22)
         c) Human Wisdom Is Devilish (vv. 19–20)
   B. The Power of God with the Power of Man (v. 24)
      1. The Power of God (v. 18)
         a) The Power by Which Christ Came
         b) The Power by Which Christ Lived
         c) The Power by Which Christ Died
         d) The Power by Which Christ Rose
         e) The Power by Which Christ Saves
      2. The Power of Man (v. 22)
         a) The Scientific Approach to Things Spiritual Is Inadequate
         b) The Scientific Approach to Things Spiritual Is Impertinent
II. The Christian Message Is God's Redemptive Invitation to Man (v. 24)
   A. God's Pleasure in the Invitation of the Gospel (v. 21)
   B. God's Purpose in the Invitation of the Gospel (v. 18)
   C. God's Process in the Invitation of the Gospel (vv. 21, 24)

chapter TWO

THE CHARACTER
OF THE CHRISTIAN MESSAGE

In our last study we considered "The Contradiction of the Christian Message" as reflected in a divided and, therefore, defeated church. By way of contrast, we now turn to a subject of infinite wealth and worth, "The Character of the Christian Message." Let us examine 1 Corinthians 1:18–25.

> For the message of the cross is foolishness to those who are perishing, but to us who are being saved it is the power of God. For it is written: "I will destroy the wisdom of the wise, and bring to nothing the understanding of the prudent." Where is the wise? Where is the scribe? Where is the disputer of this age? Has not God made foolish the wisdom of this world? For since, in the wisdom of God, the world through wisdom did not know God, it pleased God through the foolishness of the message preached to save those who believe. For Jews request a sign, and Greeks seek after wisdom; but we preach Christ crucified, to the Jews a stumbling block and to the Greeks foolishness, but to those who are called, both Jews and Greeks, Christ the power of God and the wisdom of God.

Because the foolishness of God is wiser than men, and the weakness of God is stronger than men.

As we address these verses it is my prayer that young and old alike will discover, with a new sense of wonder, the character of the Christian message. The times may change on earth, but the truth is forever settled in heaven. We need to understand the days of revolution, or change, in which we live. This helps us to be intelligent and relevant in our presentation of the gospel. So before we come to the exposition and application of this next section of the epistle, let us briefly survey the contemporary scene.

Some time ago, a penetrating writer made some observations that were striking and significant. He pointed out that we are living in the revolution of a spiraling technology. No thoughtful person can witness the advances being made in the field of technology without feeling somewhat apprehensive. Some very exciting things are happening, but there are others that are disturbing. We know, for instance, that we have the potential to wipe out the human race. And we are told that within a matter of years it will be possible to determine breeding patterns and design all types of people within our society. Quite naturally, we cannot reflect on facts like these without becoming a little frightened.

We are living in the revolution of a rising expectation. What is publicized on Madison Avenue today is what we expect to acquire at once. Failure to realize this has become one of the most frustrating problems of our day. Everything is instant: instant tea, instant coffee, instant wealth. People become impatient when they do not get what is advertised. Moreover, what is true of the advertisements that we read in the newspapers, hear on the radio, and see on television is equally true of the promises that are made by politicians, employers, teachers, and even parents. This is an age of expectation, and old and young have become intolerant when there is a delay in personal and practical fulfillment.

We are living in the revolution of an emerging generation. While a generation gap has existed in every century, there is something quite different about the present situation. Through mass communication and modern education, young people seem to have grown up overnight. Distinctions that existed before between parents and their children have now become issues to fight about. In this emerging generation there is no longer a threat to moral authority on the basis of revolutionism but rather on the ground of relativism. Today we are told that there are no absolutes. Therefore, such terms as discipline, devotion, and commitment are symbols of an establishment that must be overthrown.

We are living in the revolution of a changing culture. Culture is the public expression of national mentality and morality. To thoughtful people, it is quite obvious that our mentality is explosive and our morality is permissive. Our mentality is explosive because we are living in a day of interrogation and investigation. Children, young people, and adults are asking questions about everything. They want answers to such burning issues as racism, hunger, oppression, pollution, population explosion, and so on. "We want answers," they say. "Don't talk to us in clichés; don't give us pious jargon. We want real answers." No longer can we silence the voices that protest and cry out against the injustices and indecisions of our time. But alongside of this is a permissive morality. Through the preaching of what Dietrich Bonhoeffer called "cheap grace" our liberal theologians have created a climate of antinomianism, not only within the church, but in society as a whole. Situation ethics has become a way of life. The Ten Commandments, once an unalterable charter for personal and national behavior, are now relative in terms of their application to modern life. We are told to regard the Ten Commandments as a rule of thumb for human convenience rather than divine insistence. We are informed that God's laws should be read as follows: "Thou shalt not take the name of the Lord thy God in vain *ordinarily*. Thou shalt not commit adultery *ordinarily*. Thou shalt not steal *ordinarily*. Thou shalt not bear false witness against thy neighbor *ordinarily*," and this, in turn, has led to unbelievable permissiveness in our society. Fornication, adultery, homosexuality, lesbianism, sodomy, pornography, and nudity are all part of the changing culture, and we are expected to tolerate all this in the interests of so-called beauty and art forms for human appreciation.

But most serious of all, we are living in the revolution of declining religion. All societies throughout the ages have asked two basic questions. The first is "Why?" and the second is "Why not?" Up until now people have turned instinctively to religion for answers to these questions; but, alas, we live in an hour when instead of answering these questions the church herself is asking them! One cynical professor has remarked, "What was once a question 'Why?' has now become an answer 'Why not?'" Dr. James Packer has asserted that "at no time, perhaps, since the Reformation have Protestant Christians as a body been so unsure, tentative, and confused as to what they should believe and do."[1]

Dr. Gene Edward Veith relates the old "Battle for the Bible" to a new "Battle for the Gospel," one being waged even in evangelical churches:

> Astonishingly, the attacks on the gospel are coming from the ranks of evangelicals themselves. Classical Protestantism has always taught that Jesus Christ died to save sinners, but many contemporary evangelicals are downplaying sin, salvation, and the Atonement. The new gospel replaces salvation with therapy. Sin

gives way to self-esteem; the doctrine of justification by faith is replaced with the doctrine of positive thinking. This new version of Christianity recasts the Bible from the Word of salvation into a step-by-step manual for happy living. The hard edges of historic Christianity—the Bible's stern moral demands, unpleasant doctrines such as Hell, Christ as the one way to salvation—are minimized in an effort to reduce Christianity to a feel-good religion. The focus of the new theology is not God, but the self. Objective doctrines are replaced by subjective experiences; worshiping a holy God gives way to entertaining the congregation. Such notions may promote church growth, but they are not historic Christianity. . . .

At issue in both the "Battle for the Bible" and the "Battle for the Gospel" is the truth of God's Word. The modernists questioned whether what the Bible said corresponded to the canons of scientific and rationalist truth. Today, we face a different dilemma. The modernist trust in science and reason has fallen apart. The postmodernists are questioning not only whether the Bible is objectively true; they are questioning whether there is any objective truth whatsoever.

Christianity, on the contrary, rests on truth. To be sure, our fallen human nature can never comprehend truth fully, and our reason by itself is incapable of knowing God's truth. This is why we need Scripture, God's self-revelation in human language, to understand our lost condition and God's gracious gift of salvation through the Cross of Jesus Christ. As Luther says in his *Large Catechism,* in a passage that refutes the claim that the Reformers and Protestant confessions did not teach the inerrancy of Scripture, "God

does not lie. My neighbor and I—in short, all men—
may err and deceive, but God's Word cannot err."[2]

It is in such a context and climate as this that we are privi-
leged to present a gospel that is both timely and timeless!
No passage in the New Testament more clearly delineates
"The Character of the Christian Message" than the verses
before us.

The first main heading is: *The Christian message is God's
distinctive revelation to mankind.* "For the message of the cross
is foolishness to those who are perishing, but to us who are
being saved it is the power of God" (v. 18). Paul's emphasis
here is not so much on the presentation of the gospel but on
the *Logos,* the word of the gospel, in contradistinction to the
"wisdom of the words" mentioned in verse 17. His supreme
objective is to point out the uniqueness of the gospel as a
revelation of the *wisdom* and *power* of God. These two words
were highly significant in the generation in which Paul
wrote. The Greeks were ever seeking after wisdom, while
the Jews were obsessed with power. Thus Paul delineates the
distinctive character of the gospel by contrasting the wisdom
of God with the wisdom of man and then the power of God
with the power of man.

First of all, the wisdom of God with the wisdom of man—
"Christ . . . the wisdom of God" (v. 24). This mighty
evangelist, this great preacher of the gospel, leaves no doubt
as to what he means by the wisdom of God. Verse 30 says,
"But . . . in Christ Jesus, who became for us wisdom from
God; and righteousness and sanctification and redemption."
The American Standard Version renders this as follows,
"Christ Jesus, who was made unto us wisdom from God,
and righteousness and sanctification, and redemption." In
other words, the wisdom of God is revealed in righteousness,
sanctification, and redemption. And in this world of synthesis

and syncretism, it is supremely important that we understand what God has to offer. We must realize afresh that religion (in the natural sense) is a person's attempt to seek after God, whereas revelation (in the spiritual sense) is God's arrival to seek after a person.

In the wisdom of God we have, first of all, the revelation of Christ as our righteousness: "But . . . in Christ Jesus, who became for us . . . righteousness" (v. 30). In and through the Lord Jesus Christ, if we have repented toward God and put our faith in Jesus as Savior, we can be made just before a holy God. This aspect of the gospel answers the ancient question, "How then can man be righteous before God?" (Job 25:4). Because the Lord Jesus Christ died for our sins and rose again for our justification (Rom. 4:25), we can know the righteousness of God imputed to us. The only message that can make a man right is the gospel. God starts with the individual because, as Professor Samuel Zwemer says, "The person who goes out to change society is an optimist, but the person who goes out to change society without changing the individual is a lunatic." God starts at the center and moves to the circumference. He makes a person right with his or her Creator and then with that person's neighbor.

Next, we have the revelation of Christ as our sanctification: "But . . . in Christ Jesus, who became for us . . . sanctification" (v. 30). We could never attain holiness in our own strength, but through the Savior's indwelling, sanctification is accomplished in us day by day. This continuous work of grace sets us apart for the purpose of God in terms of Christian belief and behavior. It means living out experimentally what we are essentially in Christ. This is the heart of our gospel. Stated simply, it means that you and I cannot live the Christian life. Indeed, it is impossible to live the Christian life. Nobody has ever lived it save the Lord Jesus Christ. But when we come in utter bankruptcy and fling ourselves at the foot of the cross, saying, "Nothing in my hand I bring, simply to Thy cross I cling," the Lord Jesus not only cleanses us by His precious blood and reconciles us to His Father-God, but He communicates to us His resurrection life by the Holy Spirit. So a wonderful thing happens: we become new creatures; old things pass away, all things become new, and we are indwelt by the saving life of Christ. He looks through our eyes, speaks through our lips, works through our hands, walks through our feet, loves through our hearts, works out His purpose through our human personalities, and we discover that there is no demand made upon our lives that is not a demand upon His life in us. What a gospel!

Then we have the revelation of Christ as our redemption: "But . . . in Christ Jesus, who became for us . . . redemption" (v. 30). This word means *release* or *deliverance*. In this particular context it is not only redemption from the penalty and power of sin but from the very presence of sin. It is the final act of God by which we are made to conform to Christ in all the wonder of His likeness and glory. This final act could happen before the close of this day! I feel that we are on the verge of that great event. What a wonderful thought!

This, then, is the distinctive revelation of God to mankind, namely, Christ our righteousness, our sanctification, our redemption. But this revelation is wholly outside of a person's capacity to conceive or perceive what God has prepared for those who love Him. Only the Holy Spirit can interpret to us the wonder of this Christian message in all its faithfulness and fullness.

Now Paul turns to the wisdom of man: "For since, in the wisdom of God, *the world through wisdom did not know God*" (v. 21). This means that the world by philosophy and sophistry cannot know God. The apostle Paul agrees with the writer James when he tells us that human wisdom is "earthly, sensual, demonic" (3:15). Let us interpret this evaluation of human wisdom and see how Paul and James concur.

Human wisdom is earthly: "For since, in the wisdom of God, the world through wisdom did not know God" (v. 21). Paul is telling us that human wisdom is bound by limitation; it is earthly. Indeed, he states that God in His wisdom has decreed that the world by human wisdom cannot know God. This forever annihilates the notion that a person by his or her own reasoning or intellectual attainments can find God, let alone *know* God! Human education at its highest and best is hardly adequate. No wonder the French scientist and religious philosopher, Blaise Pascal, once exclaimed, "The supreme achievement of reason is to bring us to see that there is a limit to reason."

Human wisdom is earthly, but it is also sensual. This is why Paul, with a touch of irony, says, "The Greeks seek after wisdom." William Barclay reminds us that

> originally the Greek word *sophist* meant "a wise man" in the good sense; but later it came to signify a man with a clever mind and cunning tongue, a mental acrobat, a man who with glittering and persuasive rhetoric could make the worst appear the better reason. . . . It meant a man who gloried in a nimble and cunning brain and in a silver tongue and in an admiring audience.

What was true of Paul's day is still true today. There is nothing that appeals to the sensual and carnal person like the so-called intellectual speaker, the sophisticated preacher, or the silver-tongued orator, simply because such a communicator can pour out torrents of high-sounding words that mesmerize people by sheer rhetoric. Young people, particularly, run hither and thither after such people instead of sticking to the bread-and-butter issues of the gospel of our Lord Jesus Christ.

Human wisdom is earthly, human wisdom is sensual, but even more importantly, human wisdom is devilish. So Paul quotes God as saying: "I will destroy the wisdom of the wise, and bring to nothing the understanding of the prudent. Where is the wise? Where is the scribe? Where is the disputer of this age? Has not God made foolish the wisdom of this world?"(vv. 19–20). Human wisdom is described as devilish because it is associated with the devil who fell by pride. There is nothing more abhorrent to God than philosophical arrogance or intellectual snobbery. Every movement that has undermined the authority of the Scriptures, call it what you will—modernism, liberalism, existentialism, humanism, or postmodernism—is all part of this philosophical approach; and because of human pride, men seek to be identified with the famous names of these schools of thought in order to secure status. But God calls it devilish.

Many years ago my heart was deeply stirred by the testimony of Mr. A. Lindsay Gregg of London, England (then in his nineties). Standing before a breathless throng of young and old he told how, as a university student, he was carried away by the preaching and teaching of a minister who had left the impregnable rock of Holy Scripture for the sands of philosophical speculation, and how God, in love and mercy, drew him back to Himself, back to the Word, back to the church, and back to Christian service. I thought of young people across America, Britain, and the rest of the world as he concluded with these words: "Read the Bible, keep at the foot of the cross, keep close to your Savior. Make much of His virgin birth, His Deity, His sinless life, His atoning death, His indisputable resurrection, His High Priestly ministry, His certain return as Judge and Lord of all." But somebody says, "If you talk like that and believe like that are you not committing intellectual suicide?" The answer is no, for with Pascal we must remember that "the supreme achievement of reason is to bring us to see that there is a limit to reason." Once we arrive at this point and submit to divine revelation, *we then begin to use our reasoning powers as never before.* Then and only then can our minds be stretched and strengthened by the Holy Spirit to understand things from God's point of view.

So we have seen what Paul means by God's distinctive revelation to men in terms of wisdom. Having compared the wisdom of God with the wisdom of man, Paul now proceeds to contrast the power of God with the power of man. Look at verse 24: "Christ the power of God." To understand the distinct contrast between the power of God and the power of man it is necessary for us to examine carefully the meaning behind Paul's use of these phrases. Consider first the power of God. "The message of the cross . . . to us who are being saved . . . is the power of God" (v. 18). When God brought creation into being He only had to speak a word, but when God brought redemption to pass He had to send His only begotten Son. So the expression "the power of God" comprehends the total act of God in Christ by which He made redemption possible for a world of ruined sinners.

Think of the power by which Christ came. The incarnation of our Lord Jesus Christ was a supernatural act of God. This is clear from the words of the angel to Mary, "The Holy Spirit will come upon you, and the power of the Highest will overshadow you; therefore, also, that Holy One who is to be born will be called the Son of God" (Luke 1:35). We observe, then, that it took nothing less than the exceeding might of divine power to effect this mystery of godliness. This is why I believe in the virgin birth.

But with the power by which Christ came, consider the power by which Christ lived. The life of our Lord Jesus here upon earth was a supernatural act of God. Paul tells us that "Jesus Christ our Lord . . . was . . . declared to be the Son of God with power according to the Spirit of holiness, by the resurrection from the dead" (Rom. 1:3–4). His sinless life is one of the greatest phenomena of the ages. I believe in His sinless life.

Then there is the power by which Christ died. The death of Christ was a supernatural act of God, for let us remember that when Jesus Christ hung upon the cross He was made sin for us in order that "we might become the righteousness of God in Him" (2 Cor. 5:21). Then having completed His divine mission He voluntarily bowed His head and gave up His Spirit. No one ever died like that. This is why Paul says, "The [word] of the cross is . . . the power of God" (v. 18). I believe in His atoning death.

Next is the power by which Christ rose. The resurrection of the Savior was a supernatural act of God. The apostle speaks of "the exceeding greatness of [God's] power . . . which He worked in Christ when He raised Him from the dead" (Eph. 1:19–20). The resurrection of Christ is the foundation stone of Christian doctrine, it is the Gibraltar of Christian evidence, it is the Waterloo of infidelity and rationalism. If Christ did not rise from the dead our faith would be vain and we, of all men, would be most miserable. So I believe in the triumphant resurrection of Christ.

Finally, there is the power by which Christ saves. The salvation of a sinner is a supernatural act of God. This is why Paul declares, "I am not ashamed of the gospel of Christ, for it is the power of God to salvation for everyone who believes, for the Jew first and also for the Greek" (Rom. 1:16). At the very heart of the gospel is the dynamic of God to save and to deliver. There is nothing else in all the universe that can transform the human life like the gospel of our Lord Jesus Christ.

I cannot read Romans 1:16 without seeing a long-haired fellow named David, thirty years of age. He had been married twice, divorced twice. He had mainlined until his arms and legs were black and blue, but drugs had not satisfied him, and so he turned to alcohol until he became a complete outcast, even though he was the son of a Moody Bible Institute-trained father and mother. One night he "chanced" upon a TV program where "Jesus People" were being interviewed. He was so impressed with the joy and fervency of these recent converts to Christ that he longed to share their faith, so the following Sunday he turned on his TV, hoping to see something similar. Instead, however, he saw six lesbians and heard them tell of their sordid experiences. Even in his degraded state he could not take this, so he switched to another program that, in God's providence, was my own gospel presentation called ENCOUNTER. Through this means he was gloriously saved and was trained for Christian service. Only the gospel could do that!

If that is the power of God, let us dwell for a moment on the power of man. "The Jews," says Paul, "request a sign" (v. 22), and, as Dr. Leon explains, this insistence on scientific proof has been characteristic of the Hebrew people throughout their history. They have shown little interest in speculative thought; their demand has been for evidence. They have thought of God as manifesting Himself in history through miracles and wonders. This is why the Jews were forever seeking signs from our Lord during His earthly ministry. They conceived of the Messiah as One who demonstrated His authority by manifestations of power and majesty. To them, a crucified Christ was a contradiction in terms.[3]

This, of course, illustrates perfectly the so-called scientific method that proceeds from observation through experimentation to demonstration. People tell us that

Christian supernaturalism must be rejected because it is inconsistent and incompatible with scientific knowledge. Such an outlook is both inadequate and impertinent. The apostle affirms this in a classic passage in Romans 10 when he says:

But the righteousness of faith speaks in this way,

> Do not say in your heart, "Who will ascend into heaven?" (that is, to bring Christ down from above) or, "Who will descend into the abyss?" (that is, to bring Christ up from the dead). But what does it say? "The word is near you, in your mouth and in your heart" (that is, the word of faith which we preach): that if you confess with your mouth the Lord Jesus and believe in your heart that God has raised Him from the dead, you will be saved. (vv. 6–9)

In other words, a human being cannot lift a little finger to bring Christ down from heaven, nor can he or she do any more to raise Christ from the grave. God has had to take the initiative at every stage of the sinner's redemption. This is why the gospel is unique; and this is why the scientific approach to spiritual things is wholly inadequate.

But more than this, the scientific approach to spiritual things is truly impertinent. So the apostle asks the stinging question, "Who has known the mind of the LORD that he may instruct Him?" (1 Cor. 2:16). And in another place the apostle exclaims, "Who are you to reply against God? Will the thing formed say to him who formed it, 'Why have you made me like this?'" (Rom. 9:20).

So we see that the revelation of the gospel is not only beyond man's philosophical approach but also beyond man's scientific method. Once a seeking soul has reached this point he is ready for the second characteristic of the gospel of our

Lord Jesus Christ. My first point was that the Christian message is God's distinctive revelation to man; the second is that *the Christian message is God's redemptive invitation to man.* "But to those who are called, both Jews and Greeks, Christ the power of God and the wisdom of God" (v. 24). Here we see presented the perfect balance of the gospel. God not only gives us a revelation of Himself, He also gives an invitation to Himself. This is more than human wisdom; this is more than human power.

Consider first God's pleasure in the invitation of the gospel: "It pleased God through the foolishness of the message preached to save those who believe" (v. 21). Paul tells us here that the supreme pleasure of God, or more literally, God's good pleasure, is that men and women should be brought to a saving knowledge of Himself through preaching. Observe carefully that it is God who takes the initiative. The picture is not of man searching after God, but rather God seeking after man in all his lostness. Ever since Adam bowed to the voice of personified sin, God, in grace, has been asking, "Adam where are you?"

Furthermore, there is God's purpose in the invitation of the gospel: "For the message of the cross is foolishness to those who are perishing, but to us who are being saved it is the power of God" (v. 18). Let us remember that every person out of Christ is lost. Indeed, the verb rendered *perish* in verse 18 denotes not extinction but ruin and loss of well-being. A person who is perishing fails to fulfill the purpose for which God created him, but this is where the gospel of the Lord Jesus Christ meets him and saves him unto eternal life. The idea behind this word *saved* is not only that of reclamation but also of transformation.

Then there is the process of God in the invitation of the gospel. Not only His pleasure, not only His purpose, but the process of God in the invitation of the gospel: "It pleased

God through the foolishness of the message preached to save
those who believe . . . . but to those who are called . . . Christ
the power of God and the wisdom of God" (vv. 21, 24).
There are two words that sum up the divine process in the
invitation of the gospel. One is the word *called,* and the other
is the word *believe.* One describes the offer of God: He calls;
it is His effectual call. The other denotes the response of
people: they believe, they commit themselves. Jesus is always
calling men and women to Himself, and, thank God, out of
every tribe, tongue, and nation people are responding. Wherever the Holy Spirit works and woos, men and women respond. That is the glorious process: God calls, and people
believe. I am glad that God called me to be an evangelist!
There is nothing more thrilling in all the world than to issue the call of the gospel and to see men and women believe.
So we observe that this redemptive invitation of God demands a verdict. A person can never confront the gospel of
the Lord Jesus Christ and remain indifferent, apathetic, or
aloof. He or she has to decide. With the revelation and invitation of the gospel a person has to give an answer. If he believes, he is saved; if she rejects, she is lost.

The Corinthian believers were divided because they had
false notions concerning this glorious message of the gospel.
This is why Paul takes pains in this first paragraph to set forth
the character of the evangel. And having treated his subject
thoroughly, he concludes with these words, "The foolishness
of God is wiser than men, and the weakness of God is
stronger than men" (v. 25). In effect, he says that the
philosophies and power demonstrations of men may come
and go, but the gospel of Jesus Christ is unchanged and
unchanging.

I am reminded of the occasion when Carl F. H. Henry,
the editor-in-chief of *Christianity Today,* attended a press
conference called by Dr. Karl Barth. Dr. Henry asked the

famous theologian how he would have written up the event of the resurrection of Jesus Christ had he been one of the early apostles. Stung by the question, Karl Barth played for time by snapping back with the demand, "What religious journal do you represent?" The answer was swift and simple, *"Christianity Today."* "No," retorted Barth, "you mean 'Christianity Yesterday.'" Without hesitation, however, and with anointed insight, Henry countered with these choice words: "You're wrong, sir, it is rather, 'Christianity Yesterday, and Today, and Forever'!"

How wonderful to know that even though times may change truth is changeless and unchanging! Our gospel is the same yesterday, today, and forever. Hallelujah!

1 Corinthians 1:26-31

I. God Selects His Community of Witnessing Saints
    Through the Simplicity of the Christian Message (v. 26).
    A. The Selective Simplicity of the Gospel Does Not
        Appeal to Many People of Intellectual Attainments
        (v. 26)
    B. The Selective Simplicity of the Gospel Does Not
        Appeal to Many People of Influential Achievements
        (v. 26)
    C. The Selective Simplicity of the Gospel Does Not
        Appeal to Many People of Intersocial Advancements
        (v. 26)
II. God Elects His Community of Witnessing Saints
     Through the Supremacy of the Christian Message
     (vv. 27–28)
     A. God Has Chosen to Save Foolish Humanity (v. 27)
     B. God Has Chosen to Save Feeble Humanity (v. 27)
     C. God Has Chosen to Save Fallen Humanity (v. 27)
III. God Protects His Community of Witnessing Saints
     Through the Sufficiency of the Christian Message (v. 30)
     A. Righteousness to Cover Our Past (v. 30)
     B. Sanctification to Cope with Our Present (v. 30)
     C. Redemption to Care for Our Future (v. 30)

chapter THREE

THE COMMUNITY
OF THE CHRISTIAN MESSAGE

The Christian message is not an intangible ideology. It is essentially the Word of God incarnate. The apostle John makes this clear in the magnificent prologue to his gospel. He says, "In the beginning was the Word, and the Word was with God, and the Word was God" (John 1:1). We would not know anything about God save for that Word. But for that Word to become humanly comprehensible it had to be fleshed out. So we read, "And the Word became flesh and dwelt among us, and we beheld His glory, the glory as of the only begotten of the Father, full of grace and truth" (John 1:14). Mark carefully the clarity and symmetry of this interpersonal revelation. Grace reflects the curved lines of revelation while truth projects the straight lines. Here we see the glory of divine artistry. We need grace and truth to have the perfect balance, and in "the only begotten of the Father" (John 1:14), we have this perfect balance of love and light. As one theologian has put it, "Jesus Christ [became] God's conversation with men." This was God's climactic intervention into community life upon earth. What happened vertically is now being worked out horizontally by God's Spirit through people like you and me. This is the community of the Christian message.

Notice the imperative mood in 1 Corinthians 1:26–31:

> For you see your calling, brethren, that not many wise according to the flesh, not many mighty, not many noble, are called. But God has chosen the foolish things of the world to put to shame the wise, and God has chosen the weak things of the world to put to shame the things which are mighty; and the base things of the world and the things which are despised God has chosen, and the things which are not, to bring to nothing the things that are, that no flesh should glory in His presence. But of Him you are in Christ Jesus, who became for us wisdom from God; and righteousness and sanctification and redemption; that, as it is written, "He who glories, let him glory in the LORD."

The apostle is still dealing with the problem of division in the church. So he proceeds to show how strife and contention can result not only from wrong notions concerning the character of the message of the gospel but also from wrong ideas concerning the community of the Christian message. In His divine sovereignty and inscrutable wisdom, God has so designed the appeal of the gospel that we can merit absolutely nothing by responding to it. For this reason the community of the Christian message consists of a company of men and women who have learned that "no flesh should glory in His presence" (v. 29). No truly redeemed person can stand up and say, "See who I am"; instead, he kneels to confess that "Jesus Christ is Lord, to the glory of God the Father" (Phil. 2:11). God wants the world to see the glory of His Son through a community of saints in radiating beams of grace and truth.

It was because of the failure of the Corinthian Christians

to see this that they were vying one against the other under the banners of their respective leaders. So Paul sets out to show that this problem can only be solved when people understand God's method of selecting, electing, and protecting the community of believers in Jesus Christ.

It is important, especially for some of our younger friends, to recognize that the community of believers is, in fact, *the church*. We are living in an hour when people are saying that the greatest stumbling block to understanding the Christian message is the church! These people say, "We want Jesus, but we don't want the church." You see how confused men and women have become! They see a dichotomy between Christ and the church, but there is no such dichotomy, for Christ is the Head of the church, and Christ calls the church His own Body. When Saul of Tarsus persecuted the church of Jesus Christ he was stricken down by a brilliant light, above the brightness of the meridian sun, and he heard a voice from heaven affirming, "I am Jesus, whom you are persecuting" (Acts 9:5). What the Lord Jesus was saying was, "Every Christian you are persecuting, every Christian you are imprisoning, every Christian you are causing to blaspheme is part of my Body, and *you are hurting Me*" (see Acts 9, 22, 26).

We need to be very careful, therefore, when we talk about the church, for while there are many things about the dead, cold, and irrelevant establishment that we must criticize and correct, there is great caution required lest we actually insult or injure the very Body of Christ. If we are redeemed at all by the blood of Christ, if we are quickened at all by the Spirit of God, if we are taught at all by the Word of truth, then we are part of the church. Jesus said, "And I also say to you that you are Peter, and on this rock I will build My church, and the gates of Hades shall not prevail against it" (Matt. 16:18). There is a future for the church, and although her critics may come and go, the church of Jesus Christ will endure forever.

Let us return to the verses we read earlier and consider that *God selects His community of witnessing saints through the simplicity of the Christian message.* "For you see your calling, brethren, that not many wise according to the flesh, not many mighty, not many noble, are called" (v. 26). Later on in his second epistle, Paul expresses a fear "lest somehow . . . the serpent . . . by his craftiness, so [corrupt the Corinthians'] minds . . . from the simplicity that is in Christ" (2 Cor. 11:3). The reason why people are being turned away from the church today is because so many Christians have ceased to be simple in their commitment to and contentment in Christ. This is why Paul invites us to survey the church and observe that those who constitute its membership are, for the most part, simple people.

The selective simplicity of the gospel does not appeal to many people of intellectual attainments: "Not many wise according to the flesh . . . are called" (v. 26). This is not because Christianity is anti-intellectual, as we shall see later, but because there is a natural tendency in the unregenerate person to *think* independently of God, as we observed so clearly in our last study. This is why the Lord Jesus declared, "Unless you are converted and become as little children, you will by no means enter the kingdom of heaven" (Matt. 18:3). And on another occasion He looked up to heaven and said, "I thank You, Father, Lord of heaven and earth, that You have hidden these things from the wise [the philosophical] and prudent [the sophisticated] and have revealed them to babes. Even so, Father, for so it seemed good in Your sight" (Matt. 11:25–26). Heaven has decreed that people by their wisdom, their philosophy, and their knowledge, cannot know God. This unqualified repudiation of the philosophical approach to eternal things is in order "that no flesh should glory in His presence" (v. 29). Nobody will ever be able to say, "Thank God I am in heaven because my brain has brought me here." The selective simplicity of the gospel does not appeal to many people of intellectual attainments. They have to repent; they have to change their thinking and submit to God's way of salvation.

It is also clear that the selective simplicity of the gospel does not appeal to many people of influential achievements: "Not many mighty . . . are called" (v. 26). There is a natural tendency in the unregenerate not only to think independently of God but to work independently of God. The word "mighty" is a term used of people who have gained a place of influence through their own achievements. Unless this pride of influence is "crucified with Christ," trouble is always lurking in the church.

We are all familiar with a character in the church of Ephesus who caused unspeakable heartache. His name was Diotrephes, and his love of preeminence created nothing but strife and contention (3 John 9–11). Indeed, because of his place of influence he had attacked the apostle John with "malicious words." In fact, there are scholars who tell us he had actually intercepted a letter to the Ephesian church. There is also a strong implication that he had tried to rival the authority of the aged and loved apostle. All this serves to illustrate the corrupting influence of uncrucified power, and for this reason "not many mighty . . . are called" (v. 26). God has willed it so "that no flesh should glory in His presence" (v. 29). Nobody can say when he gets to heaven, "I came here by means of my own works." The Bible says, "Not by works of righteousness which we have done, but according to His mercy He saved us" (Titus 3:5).

Again, the selective simplicity of the gospel does not appeal to many people of intersocial advancements: "Not many noble, are called" (v. 26). There is a natural tendency in the unregenerate person to *live* independently of God. Most commentators are agreed that the word "noble" applies to family connections and indicates those of high social standing. While there are outstanding exceptions, very few people of noble rank ever seem to be attracted by the Christian message.

In Paul's day, as in every age, there were the exceptions. There were such great personalities as Dionysius and Damaris of Athens (Acts 17:34), Sergius Paulus, proconsul of Cyprus (Acts 13:7), the noble ladies of Thessalonica and Berea (Acts 17:4, 12), and not least, of course, the apostle himself, who were called into the fellowship of God's Son. Since then we could talk about a host of others, people like Count Zinzendorf and Madame Guyon, who came from nobility. Lady Huntingdon, an English woman of great distinction who was converted under the preaching of Rowland Hill, the evangelist, once remarked that she owed her salvation to the letter "m." She explained that if the text had read, "Not *any* wise . . . not *any* mighty, and not *any* noble" she could never have been saved. But the text does not say "any," it reads "not *many*"! There have been some noble people saved in the past, and there will be others in the future, until the church of Jesus Christ is complete; but the fact remains that the simplicity of the gospel does not appeal to those of intersocial advancements. Once again, God has willed it so in order "that no flesh should glory in His presence" (v. 29).

Anyone with a knowledge of the congregational life of a church will know that contention and division are often caused by the desire and determination of some to have human recognition. It is only when we realize that we cannot think or work or live apart from God that true humility and consequent harmony come into the local fellowship. May the Spirit of God teach us to say and mean:

Naught have I gotten but what I received;
Grace hath bestowed it since I have believed.

James M. Gray

This further brings us to see that *God elects His community of witnessing saints through the supremacy of the Christian message.* "God has chosen the foolish things of the world to put to shame the wise, and God has chosen the weak things of the world to put to shame the things which are mighty; and the base things of the world and the things which are despised God has chosen, and the things which are not, to bring to nothing the things that are" (vv. 27–28). To teach men and women that no flesh should glory in His presence, God has designed that His electing grace should demonstrate the utter supremacy of the gospel. So, God has chosen to save foolish humanity—"God has chosen the *foolish* things of the world to put to shame the wise" (v. 27). The word Paul employs to describe humanity is one from which we derive our term *moron.* It is a word that means "sluggish," "silly," or "stupid." But in His grace, God takes material like this and transforms it by the redeeming work of Christ, so as to confound the wise of this world. Human philosophy can never explain the miracle of regeneration. The psychologist may attempt his analysis, the doctor his diagnosis, the scientist his experimentation, but ultimately all are confounded by the life-changing power of the gospel.

Some years ago after our Sunday evening evangelistic service at Calvary Baptist Church, New York City, a distinguished gentleman sought me out and asked if he could have a word with me. We sat down and he began: "What you have had to say tonight has made sense. It is both reasonable and acceptable and I must act upon it. I want the Lord Jesus Christ to come into my life. I desperately need Him." I did not even ask his name. I opened my Bible, expounded the way of salvation, and told him that the genius of the Christian message is that what we cannot do, in and of ourselves, God can do in us and through us. Christ died to make this possible, shed His blood to purge away our sins, rose again to impart His life, and stands waiting, though unseen to natural eyes, to enter our lives. And if only we invite Him He always keeps His promise. "Fair enough," admitted my friend, "I will ask Him in." We bowed our heads and he prayed a simple prayer, and in that moment Christ entered and possessed his personality.

With a smile on his face he extended his hand and was about to leave, when I asked, "Do you mind telling me who you are?" He replied, "My name is Edgar Congdon. I am a doctor." "In what field?" I inquired. Graciously my friend explained, "I started off in surgery, went into general medicine, and then I decided to become a psychiatrist." I continued, "Dr. Congdon, may I ask you why you came here tonight?" His answer was both interesting and significant. Quietly he told me how he had always carried a chip on his shoulder. He looked down on Christians as morons and nitwits, and yet all the time he knew in his heart that he was "the stupid idiot." Although thoroughly qualified to analyze patients, prescribe medication, perform operations, give shock treatments, and so on, he had to confess that he had sent hundreds of patients away from his office without the real answer, because he did not have the answer himself. But then he added with a note of triumph in his voice, *"Now I have the answer!"* God has chosen to save foolish humanity, and we have to own our foolishness before we can know His salvation.

God has chosen to save feeble humanity: "God has chosen the *weak* things of the world to put to shame the things which are mighty" (v. 27). Here is another characteristic of men and women who know nothing of the saving grace of

God. Paul speaks of them as "weak," a word that means "strengthless" or "impotent." How wonderful to know that "when we were still without strength, in due time Christ died for the ungodly" (Rom. 5:6). And again, "Not by works of righteousness which we have done, but according to His mercy He saved us, through the washing of regeneration and renewing of the Holy Spirit" (Titus 3:5). People are powerless to work out their own salvation.

Never was this more evident than in our highly civilized age of technology. Philosophy has failed to answer the great questions concerning humanity's supernatural origin, purpose on earth, and ultimate destiny. Likewise, the scientific method has proved to be totally inadequate to cope with humanity's basic problem of sin. With all the creations of our inventive minds, we have no computer and no machinery to change a person's character. If anything, we have produced more technological, psychological, and theological problems than we have been able to solve. Once again, this is where the gospel of our Lord Jesus Christ supremely triumphs by taking up the feeble and making them strong in the grace that God supplies through His eternal Son.

Notice how God has chosen to save fallen humanity: "And the base things of the world and the things which are *despised* God has chosen, and *the things which are not,* to bring to nothing the things that are" (v. 28). Here Paul introduces three expressions to describe the utter fallenness of man. "Base things" conveys the thought of that which is low-born, and therefore morally worthless; "things which are despised" signifies that which is contemptible; "things which are not" suggest the nonentities of this world. What a hopeless picture of fallen humanity! Yet the Lord Jesus by His saving cross receives and redeems such men and women and uses them to bring to naught things that are. Glory to God for such a Savior!

So we see that the word of the gospel has an instructive message for foolish humanity, a redemptive message for feeble humanity, and a creative message for fallen humanity. Out of these three types of lost people God constitutes a community of saints and a community of witnesses.

Thus we see that there is no greater commendation for or demonstration of the gospel than a person under the control of the saving life of Christ—like the old sailor who was so wonderfully converted and so visibly transformed that people kept on asking why his lifestyle was different. To answer this question he got his wife to knit him a sweater with the words "Under New Management" in bold letters on the back and front. Those three words became his "text" for a five-minute sermon on the transforming power of the gospel of Christ.

In conclusion, we observe how *God protects His community of witnessing saints through the sufficiency of the Christian message.* Paul says, "But of Him you are in Christ Jesus, who became for us wisdom from God; and righteousness and sanctification and redemption" (v. 30). For those who do respond to the selective and elective gospel there is a protective sufficiency in the gospel of Christ. The revelation of the wisdom of God, as seen in Jesus Christ, is made available to every one of us, in terms of comprehensive significance.

There is righteousness to cover our past. "Christ Jesus . . . became for us . . . righteousness" (v. 30). This means justification in Christ. We attain a standing before God impossible otherwise or elsewhere. It is the assurance of pardon for sin and peace of heart. Isn't it wonderful to know that once the righteousness of God has been imputed to us we are before Him just as if we had never sinned? As justified persons, we are made to appear before God in a favorable light, and there is no angel in heaven, no being on earth, and no devil in hell who can challenge that! Here is our acceptance and assurance in Christ. So I ask you, have you been justified? Are you right with God?

Dr. Donald Barnhouse used to tell of a message he delivered in his church in Philadelphia on what God does with our sins. He pointed out that God has put our sins into the depths of the sea; He has put our sins as far as the east is from the west; He has put our sins behind His back. At the end of the service, as he was shaking hands with members of his congregation, a little fellow with bright eyes, a sharp suit, and an impressive bow tie stood with consummate assurance before his pastor and exclaimed, "Say, Doc, on the business of our sins, we are sitting pretty, aren't we?"

But with righteousness to cover our past, there is sanctification to cope with our present: "Christ Jesus . . . became for us . . . sanctification" (v. 30). Dr. G. Campbell Morgan points out that sanctification is purification through separation.[1] It is both positional and practical. While it is true that "by one offering [God] has perfected forever those who are being sanctified" (Heb. 10:14), it is equally true that we are to "cleanse ourselves from all filthiness of the flesh and spirit, perfecting holiness [sanctification] in the fear of God" (2 Cor. 7:1). This progressive sanctification is the very life of Christ indwelling us moment by moment. And since all the fullness of the Godhead dwells bodily in our Lord Jesus Christ, there is no demand upon our lives that is not adequately met by the sufficiency that is in Him. It is our joy to rest in all that Christ has done for us, and will also do in us. Eliza H. Hamilton expresses this beautifully in those words we often sing:

> My Saviour, Thou hast offered rest:
> O give it then to me;
> The rest of ceasing from myself,
> To find my all in Thee.

Show me a satisfied Christian, show me a believer whose life is a sanctifying influence in the community, and I will show you a person who has no problem in witnessing for Christ. The apostle Peter states the same principle when he says, "Sanctify the Lord God in your hearts, and always be ready to give a defense to everyone who asks you a reason for the hope that is in you, with meekness and fear" (1 Peter 3:15).

This sanctification is not only a personal power, it is a social power. As Christians, we are the salt of the earth, we are the light of the world (Matt. 5:13–16). So whether we are in business, in politics, in the home, or in the church, we should be effecting a silent influence in society. We are the salt of the earth. But more than this, we should be effecting a vibrant radiance in society. We are the light of the world. Christians should be the strongest protesters against pornography, against nudity in films, against the moral filth and political corruption of our day. As sanctified Christians, we should be speaking by life and by lip to the burning issues of our contemporary life. I am not contending for careless, tactless, or ruthless behavior. I am not advocating unlawful assembly or the violation of other civil regulations, for we, as Christians, are to submit to every ordinance of man for the Lord's sake (1 Peter 2:13), but I am asserting that *our lives should be a challenge to everything that is wrong.*

There is, then, righteousness to cover our past, sanctification to cope with our present, and now redemption to care for our future: "Christ Jesus . . . became for us . . . redemption" (v. 30). Redemption means the final escape from all bondage. It is a word that occurs some ten times in the New Testament, and on every occasion it refers primarily to the future rather than to the present or the past. Paul is speaking of the same things when he says, "Now our salvation is nearer than when we first believed" (Rom. 13:11). This is the sense in which Christ is made unto us redemption. This is the assurance of ultimate deliverance from sin, self, and Satan. This is the day when He will fashion us into His own glorious likeness and loveliness. This is the sufficiency of the Christian message by which God protects the community of His witnessing saints.

Paul's purpose in presenting this truth was to remove forever from people's minds the thought of glorying in any other than God Himself: "That, as it is written, 'He who glories, let him glory in the LORD'" (v. 31). That which divides the church is the spirit that glories in human knowledge, glories in human influence, glories in human reputation. So the apostle has endeavored to show that no one has anything to glory of, save in the Lord Jesus Christ. We cannot think our way into salvation, we cannot work our way into salvation, we cannot live our way into salvation; we are cast on the mercy of God alone, and when we trust in Jesus we simply become the vehicles through which the grace and truth of the Son of God shine forth in a blaze of beauty and glory.

John belonged to a club where language was coarse, standards were low, and tempers were short. One day he was invited by a young man with a radiant face to his local church and then later to the Young People's Christian Fellowship. The welcome he received and the compassion he was shown deeply touched his heart. Then he heard the message of the gospel, and by exercising repentance toward God and faith in the Lord Jesus Christ he was gloriously saved and miraculously transformed. He left the club and began to attend the church, but it was not long before he was sought out by some of his old pals from the club who wanted to know why he had joined the church. John's answer was classic and conclusive. With a grin on his face and a nod towards the church, he said very simply, "They loves a feller over there." This is what Jesus meant when He said, "By this all will know that you are My disciples, if you have love for one another" (John 13:35).

The simplicity, the supremacy, and the sufficiency of our message make this possible. This is the community of the Christian message. In our acts of worship and witness within our contemporary world we can either express this community of Christian living to the glory of God, or we can eclipse the outshining of Christ to our own confusion and condemnation. God give us the grace to "walk worthy of the calling with which you were called, with all lowliness and gentleness, with longsuffering, bearing with one another in love, endeavoring to keep the unity of the Spirit in the bond of peace" (Eph. 4:1–3).

1 Corinthians 2:1-5

I. The Supreme Passion of a Communicator (vv. 1–2)
   A. Dedication to the Master (v. 2)
   B. Concentration on the Message (v. 2)
II. The Spiritual Power of a Communicator (vv. 3–4)
   A. The Power of Divine Revelation (vv. 3–4)
   B. The Power of Divine Application (vv. 3–4)
III. The Single Purpose of a Communicator (v. 5)
   A. A Sound Faith (v. 5)
   B. A Saving Faith (v. 5)
   C. A Steadfast Faith (v. 5)

THE COMMUNICATION
OF THE CHRISTIAN MESSAGE

And I, brethren, when I came to you, did not come
with excellence of speech or of wisdom declaring to
you the testimony of God. For I determined not to
know anything among you except Jesus Christ and
Him crucified. I was with you in weakness, in fear, and
in much trembling. And my speech and my preaching were not with persuasive words of human wisdom,
but in demonstration of the Spirit and of power, that
your faith should not be in the wisdom of men but in
the power of God. (1 Corinthians 2:1–5)

The Christian message, while not commending itself to
man's philosophical approach, is nevertheless the instrument
of God's power and the complement of God's wisdom. Now
Paul proceeds to discuss the communication of the message.
There is nothing more important for businessmen and
housewives, preachers, and teachers than this matter of communication. The priority program of the church until Jesus
returns is the communication of the Christian gospel to every creature in every country. The Master said, "Go therefore and make disciples of all the nations, baptizing them in

the name of the Father and of the Son and of the Holy Spirit, teaching them to observe all things that I have commanded you; and lo, I am with you always, even to the end of the age" (Matt. 28:19–20). And again, "But you shall receive power when the Holy Spirit has come upon you; and you shall be witnesses to Me in Jerusalem, and in all Judea and Samaria, and to the end of the earth" (Acts 1:8).

As a communicator himself, Paul knew something of the inherent dangers in the methods and motives of public preaching. Indeed, the church at Corinth was divided on this very issue. Some said they preferred Paul, others said they preferred Apollos, still others said they preferred Cephas, and so on. There was division because of the differences and preferences relating to the personalities and presentations of these preachers. So Paul tackles this problem by saying, in effect, that temperament, background, and training are not what matters; the power of the Holy Spirit is needed to be a communicator for Christ. This anointing of the Spirit concerns three aspects of the task as a communicator.

First of all, there is *the supreme passion of a communicator.* "And I, brethren, when I came to you, did not come with excellence of speech or of wisdom declaring to you the testimony of God. For I determined not to know anything among you except Jesus Christ and Him crucified" (vv. 1–2). Drawing heavily upon his own experience, Paul shares with us the twofold secret of the consuming passion of a gospel communicator.

To start with, there is dedication to the Master. Paul uses a special word here to describe his dedicated resolve. He says, "I *determined* not to know anything among you except Jesus Christ" (v. 2). This is the secret of a true passion for preaching and communicating. This man was so Christ-centered and Christ-controlled that nothing else mattered, save Jesus Christ. He could say, "For to me, to live is Christ" (Phil.

1:21); and again, "I also count all things loss for the excellence of the knowledge of Christ Jesus my Lord . . . that I may know Him and the power of His resurrection, and the fellowship of His sufferings, being conformed to His death" (Phil. 3:8, 10); and yet again, "One thing I do, forgetting those things which are behind and reaching forward to those things which are ahead, I press [or I pursue, the same word that he used for the persecution of the church] toward the goal for the prize of the upward call of God in Christ Jesus" (Phil. 3:13–14).

How true it is that "out of the abundance of the heart the mouth speaks" (Matt. 12:34). Some of us remember the crusade that Dr. Billy Graham had at Harringay in the city of London. I was then pastor of the Duke Street Baptist Church in Richmond, Surrey, and we took scores of people every night to the meetings. Riding home on one or two occasions by subway, I made it my business to go from car to car and meet people who had just trusted Christ. It was absolutely thrilling! These folk were so full of their newfound joy that they were singing and talking about Jesus in every compartment of the train. And it did not matter how much the conservative Britisher tried to hide his face in *The Times* or the *Telegraph,* he still had to hear. "Out of the abundance of the heart the mouth speaks" (Matt. 12:34).

Many years ago I was preaching in the city of Birmingham, England, and while there, stayed in the home of a lovely couple. Just before my arrival their daughter had become engaged, so almost the first word of greeting was, "You know, Dorothy has become engaged!" I turned to Dorothy and said, "Tell me, who is he?" and she, with radiant face, replied, "Oh, his name is George." I thought that was the end of it. But believe me when I tell you that we had George for breakfast, George for lunch, and George for supper! At the table when Dorothy passed the sugar it was with the left hand, so that everyone could see those flashing facets of the engagement ring! You see, "Out of the abundance of the heart the mouth speaks" (Matt. 12:34).

A little later, in that same city, I was speaking at a rally on the theme of witnessing, and at the close of the meeting a young fellow came to me and said, "You know, I find it difficult to speak about the Lord Jesus. I can talk about other things, but when it comes to witnessing for Christ I just seem to be tongue-tied." I paused a moment and then put this question to him, "Tell me," I asked, "have you a hobby?" "Oh, yes!" he exclaimed, "My hobby is motorcycling." "That's very interesting," I observed, "because I used to own a motorbike." His eyes opened like saucers, and in a moment he had launched into a most detailed description of motorcycles in general, and his machine in particular. In fact, for twenty minutes I couldn't get a word in edgewise! Finally I stopped him and gave him this parting word, "Son, when you spend as much time with Jesus as you do with your favorite hobby, you will have a polished twenty-minute sermon every time you speak!"

Dedication to the Master, this was Paul's passion. For him living was Christ. As the pages of the Old Testament Scriptures opened to him it was Jesus he saw. As he prayed it was Jesus he sensed. As he witnessed to others it was Jesus he shared. So it should be with us. Our holiness, our power, our victory, our blessing, are all wrapped up in Christ, and if the Lord Jesus means everything to us, we cannot but talk about Him. Thus Paul could say, "I determined not to know anything among you except Jesus Christ" (v. 2).

But alongside of dedication to the Master there was concentration on the message: "For I determined not to know anything among you except Jesus Christ *and Him crucified*" (v. 2). Paul determined to present Christ in all the simplicity of the essential facts of His death and resurrection. His supreme passion was Christ and Him crucified. And knowing what the philosophers of Corinth stood for, he saw to it that his message was Christ and Him crucified, "not in His glory but in His humiliation, that the foolishness of the preaching might be doubly foolish, and the weakness doubly weak. The incarnation was in itself a stumbling block; the crucifixion was much more than this."[1]

Some students of the Bible maintain that Paul's emphasis on the cross in the city of Corinth was because of his sense of failure in the alleged philosophical approach he adopted at Athens. But a study of Acts 17 makes it evident that the apostle's preaching there was not basically philosophical, even though he did quote from the philosophers of his day. His sermon began with a biblical presentation of creation and ended on the note of the resurrection. Why would he speak of the resurrection if there were no crucifixion? Whether in Athens or Corinth, Paul could affirm, "I determined not to know anything among you except Jesus Christ and Him crucified" (v. 2). The gospel, according to Paul, was that "Christ died for our sins according to the Scriptures . . . He was buried, and . . . He rose again the third day according to the Scriptures" (1 Cor. 15:3–4).

A young preacher in a college town was embarrassed by the thought of the criticism he was likely to receive from his cultured congregation. He sought out his father, an old and wise minister of the gospel, and said, "Father, I find it hard to outline a sermon that I can preach to these people. If I cite anything from geology, there is Doctor A, the geology professor before me. If I use an illustration from history, there is Doctor B, ready to trip me up. If I choose English literature for some allusion, I am afraid the whole English department will challenge me. What shall I do?" The sagacious and godly old man replied, "Preach the gospel, my son, they probably know very little about that!"

Tholuck, a German Lutheran theologian and evangelical preacher, adopted the motto of Count Zinzendorf, "I have only one passion, and it is He, only He." Martin Luther's preaching aroused the church from a thousand years of slumber, known by the historians as the devil's millennium. It is easy to understand why, when we discover how he preached. Luther said, "I preach as though Christ was crucified yesterday, rose again from the dead today, and is coming back to earth tomorrow." This is the supreme passion of the communicator—dedication to the Master and concentration on the message.

This brings us to our second point, which is *the spiritual power of a communicator.* "I was with you in weakness, in fear, and in much trembling. And my speech and my preaching were not with persuasive words of human wisdom, but in demonstration of the Spirit and of power" (vv. 3–4). The apostle knew that the content of his message was so unacceptable to the carnal mind that he had no confidence in his ability to communicate it. In fact, he admits that he came to Corinth "in weakness, in fear, and in much trembling" (v. 3). J. B. Phillips puts it even more dramatically when he renders Paul as saying, "I was feeling far from strong, I was nervous and rather shaky."

Have you ever felt like that as you waited in the checkout line and the lady in front of you made a remark that gave you a wide open door to witness for Christ? I am encouraged by the words of Dr. G. Campbell Morgan when he confessed that every Sunday, as he made his way to the pulpit, he was invariably reminded of that Scripture, "He was led as a lamb to the slaughter" (Isa. 53:7). I have never preached in my life without experiencing "butterflies" inside. Time and again, I have prayed, "Lord, how am I ever going to get through this message?" And instead of less fear, I was given more fear. Why? Surely it was God teaching me that it was not human oratory or human argument that was going to get the message across of a crucified and risen Savior, but rather the Holy Spirit with quiet demonstration and power. So Paul says, "I was feeling far from strong, I was nervous and rather shaky." His fear, of course, was more of God than of man. It was a fear of the task committed to him, or what Kay calls "anxious desire to fulfill his duty." Thus Paul writes, "And my speech and my preaching were not with persuasive words of human wisdom, but in demonstration of the Spirit and of power, that your faith should not be in the wisdom of men but in the power of God" (vv. 4–5). This means that Paul did not depend on what was known as "the Corinthian words" of excellent speech and poetic persuasion; his confidence, rather, was in the power of divine revelation: "I was with you . . . in demonstration of the Spirit and of power" (vv. 3–4). The word translated "demonstration" signifies "the most rigorous proof." As Dr. Leon Morris puts it, "It is possible for arguments to be logically irrefutable, yet totally unconvincing."[2]

What, then, is the secret of preaching or communicating Christ? Paul tells us that it is the demonstration of *the Spirit*. When the Holy Spirit takes over the argumentation in the simple language of a housewife, a businessman, a schoolgirl, or a schoolboy, something miraculous happens. This is the essential difference between human reasoning and divine revelation. When communicators of the Christian message trust in their own powers to convince men and women "of sin, and of righteousness, and of judgment" (John 16:8), they fail miserably, but when they trust in the Holy Spirit there is always "old-time conviction." This is why Jesus said before He left for heaven, "And when He [the Holy Spirit] has come, He will convict the world of sin, and of righteousness, and of judgment: of sin, because they do not believe in Me; of righteousness, because I go to My Father . . . of judgment, because the ruler of this world is judged" (John 16:8–11).

So we can be communicators of this glorious message of Christ and Him crucified because we have received the Spirit of revelation. Our bodies are the temples of the Holy Spirit (1 Cor. 6:19). The temple was the place of revelation, where God's word and will were made known. How wonderful to know, then, that you and I can be temples of revelation!

But there is not only the power of divine revelation, there is also the power of divine application: "I was with you . . . in demonstration [this is the revelation] of the Spirit and of power" (vv. 3–4). The phrase "of the Spirit and of power" carries us back to the "dynamic of God" in the word of the cross (1 Cor. 1:18). There is something inherent in the gospel of our Lord Jesus Christ that has a dynamic relevance, and therefore, an application to everyday living. Preach the gospel to any creature, in any country, in any age, and you will find it just as authoritative and applicable as it was in the days of the apostle Paul. I have actually spoken by interpretation, when communication involved four or five languages, and people have been converted! This is the miracle of divine application. This is why Paul exclaims, "For I am not ashamed of the gospel of Christ, for it is the power of God to salvation for everyone who believes, for the Jew first and also for the Greek" (Rom. 1:16).

A dramatic illustration of this is the young fellow I interviewed on our television program when I was a pastor in New York City. He had been one of Hell's Angels, a club of motorcycle riders. He hesitated to speak about his past life, but suffice it to say he was guilty of the most dreadful deeds of obscenity and cruelty anyone could ever talk about. Eventually, however, he came to the end of himself. He told how on a drug trip he climbed into a metal trash can, pulled the cover down, and determined to die. For four days he stayed in that self-imposed prison without light, food, or hope. Then at the urging of his mother, he attended a Billy

Graham Crusade meeting. As he lay on the grassy infield, listening to the evangelist, the withdrawal pains got worse and he began to cry; he realized he was breaking down. The Spirit of God, through revelation and application, began to communicate the message to his heart, and he decided to give his life to something greater, *Someone* who could do the job he had failed to do. Very simply, he prayed and invited Christ to take control of his life, and instantly he was delivered from the desire for drugs. Such is the power of the Holy Spirit in the revelation and application of saving truth.

My last point is *the single purpose of a communicator:* "That your faith should not be in the wisdom of men but in the power of God" (v. 5). No communicator fulfills his mission until he brings boys and girls, men and women, to rest their faith in the power of God. The power of God is nothing less than the word of the gospel, even our Lord Jesus Christ crucified and risen. The problem in Corinth was that the members of the church were seeking to pin their faith on Paul, or on Apollos, or on Cephas. So Paul takes pains to correct this divisive misplacement of confidence. To achieve this end, he realized that men and women had to exercise faith, and for faith to be sound the apostle knew that it had to be reposed in the Savior Himself without dependence on human wisdom or power. Paul amplifies this point when he writes concerning the death and resurrection of the Lord Jesus Christ in chapter 15 of this same epistle. There he declares, "If Christ is not risen, your faith is futile; you are still in your sins!" (1 Cor. 15:17). If Christ were not alive from the dead then sin was not put away, the gospel was not true, the Corinthians had believed a lie, the apostles were false witnesses, and the loved ones who had fallen asleep were gone forever. So to be sound in the faith a person must believe in the Son of God who literally and physically rose from the dead. All other tenets of evangelical faith are both included and implied in this one central and focal fact of the resurrection of Christ.

Is your faith sound? Do you believe that Jesus Christ died and rose again for your justification? Have you a sound faith? More than this, have you a saving faith? Does it stand in the power of God? Paul has explained the meaning of "the power of God" in a previous verse. He has asserted that "the message of the cross is foolishness to those who are perishing, but to us who are being saved it is the power of God" (v. 18). A saving faith is one that effects a mighty transformation in the believing soul. It is a faith that owns the Lord Jesus as Savior in the deepest sense of that word. So I ask, can you sing:

> He lives, He lives, Christ Jesus lives today!
> He walks with me and talks with me along
>   life's narrow way.
> He lives, He lives, salvation to impart!
> You ask me how I know He lives?
> He lives within my heart.
>
> *Alfred H. Ackley*

Yes, you must have a sound faith, a saving faith, and also a steadfast faith, "that your faith should not be in the wisdom of men but in the power of God" (v. 5). It has been well said that what depends upon a clever argument is at the mercy of a more clever argument. But this is not so when faith is reposed in the unchanging Son of God. This is why Paul employs the term "stand," which conveys the idea of steadfastness. Twice over in this epistle he exhorts the believer to be steadfast in the faith. The first mention follows the glorious treatment of the unalterable facts of the death and resurrection of our Lord Jesus Christ in chapter 15. Having declared the triumph of the Savior over sin and death and hell, Paul says, "Be steadfast, immovable, always abounding in the work of the Lord, knowing that your labor is not in vain in the Lord" (1 Cor. 15:58). The second reference coincides with the conclusion of the epistle where the apostle exhorts, "Watch, stand fast in the faith, be brave, be strong" (1 Cor. 16:13).

We have examined what Paul means by "The Communication of the Christian Message." He has made it abundantly plain that the gospel of God cannot be communicated or understood apart from a God-given passion, a God-given power, and a God-given purpose. Thus, whoever claims to be a communicator must possess these qualifications through the sovereign grace of the Holy Spirit.

The famous British preacher, Rowland Hill, knew something of this. Addressing the people of Wootton during one of his pastorates, he declared:

> Because I am earnest in my preaching men call me an enthusiast, a fanatic. When I first came to this part of the country I was walking on yonder hill and saw a gravel pit fall in and bury three human beings alive. I lifted up my voice for help so loudly that I was heard in the town below at a distance of nearly a mile. Help came and two of the sufferers were rescued. No one called me an enthusiast or a fanatic that day; yet when I see eternal destruction ready to fall upon poor sinners, and I call upon them to escape, men dare to call me an enthusiast and a fanatic. How little they know of my accountability to God and my responsibility to men!

Never in human history have means of communication become more accessible and adaptable to the preacher of the Christian message. Today we have the printed page, the pager, the television screen, the laptop computer, and transmission by satellite. In fact, we are told that the time will soon come when people will be able to view a television program in any part of the world by means of a device as small as a wristwatch. Such facts as these should stir our hearts and strengthen our hands as we seek to preach the Christian message to every creature. Let us remember, however, that whatever means we may employ in this technological age, nothing can ever take the place of the personal witness of life and lip. Our daily prayer should be:

> Mine are the hands to do the work;
> My feet shall run for Thee;
> My lips shall sound the glorious news:
> Lord, here am I; send me.
> *Howard W. Guinness*

1 Corinthians 2:6-16

I. Spiritual Initiation (vv. 6–7)
   A. Spiritual Birth (v. 6)
   B. Spiritual Growth (v. 7)
II. Spiritual Illumination (vv. 9–10)
   A. The Revelation of the Spirit (v. 10)
   B. The Exploration of the Spirit (v. 10)
III. Spiritual Interpretation (v. 13)
   A. The Spirit's Use of Language (v. 13)
   B. The Spirit's Terms of Reference (v. 13)
      1. The Law of Righteousness (Matt. 3:15)
      2. The Law of Yieldedness (Matt. 3:16)
      3. The Law of Prayerfulness (Luke 3:21–22)

Chapter FIVE

THE COMPREHENSION OF THE CHRISTIAN MESSAGE

However, we speak wisdom among those who are mature, yet not the wisdom of this age, nor of the rulers of this age, who are coming to nothing. But we speak the wisdom of God in a mystery, the hidden wisdom which God ordained before the ages for our glory, which none of the rulers of this age knew; for had they known, they would not have crucified the Lord of glory. But as it is written: "Eye has not seen, nor ear heard, nor have entered into the heart of man the things which God has prepared for those who love Him." But God has revealed them to us through His Spirit. For the Spirit searches all things, yes, the deep things of God. For what man knows the things of a man except the spirit of the man which is in him? Even so no one knows the things of God except the Spirit of God. Now we have received, not the spirit of the world, but the Spirit who is from God, that we might know the things that have been freely given to us by God. These things we also speak, not in words which man's wisdom teaches but which the Holy Spirit teaches, comparing spiritual things with spiritual. But the natural man does not receive the things of the Spirit of God, for they are foolishness to him; nor can he know them, because they are spiritually discerned. But he who is spiritual judges all things, yet he himself is rightly judged by no one. For "who has known the mind of the LORD that he may instruct Him?" But we have the mind of Christ. (1 Corinthians 2:6–16)

Having dealt with the content and communication of the gospel, the apostle now deals with this paragraph on "The Comprehension of the Christian Message." He anticipates those who might have inferred from his argument that the use of the intellect is not in God's economy, which is, of course, far from the truth. (For anyone in our day similarly misled I warmly commend John Stott's booklet, *The Mind Matters* [published by InterVarsity Press].) Paul deals with this issue by pointing out that the Christian message does contain philosophy, but that this system of thought is spiritual and, therefore, can only be comprehended by spiritual means.

There are three aspects of the Holy Spirit's ministry that enable us to comprehend the Christian message. The first is that of *spiritual initiation*. "However, we speak wisdom among those who are mature, yet not the wisdom of this age, nor of the rulers of this age, who are coming to nothing. But we speak the wisdom of God in a mystery, the hidden wisdom which God ordained before the ages for our glory" (vv. 6–7). In effect, Paul is saying,

Do not imagine that Christianity is devoid of philosophy, of wisdom, that it is something outside the realm of the [renewed] intellect. It is not. It has its own wisdom, its own philosophy. Indeed, what the apostle is showing here is that the Christian philosophy is the ultimate philosophy. It is *not* to be tested by other philosophies. They are to be tried by it. "We speak wisdom," he states . . . "with [absolute] finality."[1]

And the wonderful thing about it is that this ultimate wisdom of God, as revealed in Jesus Christ, is for you and me by means of divine initiation.

Paul describes this wisdom as "a mystery, the hidden wisdom which God ordained before the ages for our glory" (v. 7). It is a wisdom that comes out of eternity, invades time, and lives on throughout the ages. This is why it is called "a mystery," and therefore only comprehensible to those who are spiritually initiated. The word *mystery* signifies "something whose meaning is hidden from those who have not been initiated, but which is crystal clear to those who have."[2]

The question arises as to how you and I can be initiated, how we can be brought into this "secret of God." The answer is implicit in that little word *mature*. Paul states, "We speak wisdom among those who are *mature*" (v. 6). A careful examination of this passage makes plain that Paul equates those who are mature with those that are spiritual; in other words, those who have the Holy Spirit dwelling in them, revealing to them the deep things of God. This means, then, that spiritual initiation involves a spiritual birth followed by spiritual growth.

To start with, there must be spiritual birth: "However, we speak wisdom among those who are *mature*" (v. 6). The term *mature* denotes "the full grown" in contrast to the babe. Before there can be development and maturity there must be spiritual birth. This was an essential element in our Savior's ministry, especially when He confronted one of the most intellectual men of His day. There are scholars who inform us that this man, whose name was Nicodemus, was not only a theologian and a philosopher, he was also a scientist, for he engineered the waterworks in the city of Jerusalem! And it was to this man that the Lord Jesus said, "Most assuredly, I say to you, unless one is born again, he cannot see the kingdom of God" (John 3:3).

People say to me, "We can't understand the Bible," and invariably my answer is, "You must be born again!" If Jesus had to say to this philosopher, this theologian, this scientist, "You must be born again before you can see the kingdom of God," what about you? Thank God, this miracle can happen in your life, if only you will receive the Lord Jesus. The Bible assures us that "as many as received Him, to them He gave the right to become children of God, to those who believe in His name: who were born, not of blood, nor of the will of the flesh, nor of the will of man, but of God" (John 1:12–13). You do not enter the kingdom of God by human descent; it is "not of blood." You do not enter the kingdom of God by human desire; it is not of "the will of the flesh." You do not enter the kingdom of God by human design; it is not of "the will of man." It is rather by an act of God in response to believing faith and receiving faith. So many people believe but do not *receive*. They have been brought up in religious circles—Presbyterian churches, Methodist churches, Baptist churches, Pentecostal churches, and so on—and they have believed, but they have never received the Lord Jesus Christ. Have you received Him? Have you been born again? Only by this spiritual birth can you be initiated into the mystery of the gospel.

Spiritual birth leads to spiritual growth: "However, we speak wisdom among those who are *mature*" (v. 6). The word *mature* describes a person who has developed physically, mentally, or spiritually. In this context Paul has in mind the idea of spiritual growth. Pythagoras divided his disciples into those who were babes and those who were perfect. He made a distinction between people who had gotten beyond the rudimentary instructions in the elements of any subject and those who were still beginners. Paul makes the same distinction when he addresses the spiritual and the carnal in the third chapter, verses 1–3.

One of the heartaches in church life today is that we have so many crying, bottle-sucking spiritual babies! It is about time Christians grew up. It is about time they changed their diet from milk to meat, for "solid food belongs to those who are of full age" (Heb. 5:14). At this point it is appropriate to ask whether you have experienced this initiation of the Holy Spirit. Have you been born again, and are you growing?

But let us move on and observe that the comprehension of the Christian message involves not only spiritual initiation, but also *spiritual illumination*. "But as it is written: 'Eye has not seen, nor ear heard, nor have entered into the heart of man the things which God has prepared for those who love Him.' But God has revealed them to us through His Spirit. For the Spirit searches all things, yes, the deep things of God" (vv. 9–10). Following spiritual initiation there must be illumination, and the reason for this is that human contemplation and observation can never penetrate the deep things of God. The philosophical approach and the scientific method are limited by time and sense, and can only bring us to the end of human reasoning. But where human investigation fails, spiritual illumination prevails.

Thus Paul proceeds to show that if a person has qualified by spiritual birth and growth he can know the revelation of the Spirit: "But God has revealed [spiritual things] to us through His Spirit" (v. 10). To illustrate this point the apostle adds, "For what man knows the things of a man except the spirit of the man which is in him? Even so no one knows the things of God except the Spirit of God" (v. 11). What he is asserting is that there are certain things that only a person's spirit can know. Every one of us is aware of this. No one can really see inside our hearts and know what is there except our own spirits.

From this premise Paul goes on to argue that the same is true of God. There are deep and intimate things about God that only His Spirit can reveal to us. Or to put it in another form, there are areas of truth that the unaided human mind can never find out, save through the illumination of the Holy Spirit. This is why the Lord Jesus, when leaving His disciples, promised the Holy Spirit who would teach them all things and bring all things to their remembrance (John 14:26).

But with the revelation of the Spirit there is also the exploration of the Spirit: "For the Spirit searches all things, yes, the deep things of God" (v. 10). The function of the Holy Spirit is not only to reveal truth as it is in Christ, but also to explore truth. The word *searches* in our text is a most interesting one in the original. Herschel H. Hobbs tells us that "the term is found in ancient manuscripts for a professional searcher's report, and for the search of customs officials."[3] Just as an experienced customs official brings to light the hidden articles from a traveler's suitcase, so the Holy Spirit, in a more meaningful sense, explores the deep and hidden things of God and makes them understandable and available to the humblest Christian who is prepared to trust this indwelling Revealer and Explorer! The apostle John shares the same secret when he writes his children in the faith, "You have an anointing from the Holy One, and you know all things" (1 John 2:20).

This amazing phenomenon of spiritual revelation is what baffles the intellectuals of every age. The philosophers and scientists have been unable to understand how it is that even unlettered minds can appreciate and discuss truths that are utterly hidden from the world at large. The answer, of course, is that there is such a thing as spiritual illumination. When

Peter made that great confession concerning the Deity and Messiahship of Jesus Christ, the Master commended him with these significant words, "Simon Bar-Jonah . . . flesh and blood has not revealed this to you, but My Father who is in heaven" (Matt. 16:17).

Do you know anything about this spiritual illumination in your life? There is nothing more wonderful than to share in the revelation and exploration of the Spirit of God. Anyone who has reached this point can say with the apostle Paul, "Now we have received, not the spirit of the world, but the Spirit who is from God, that we might know the things that have been freely given to us by God" (v. 12).

But for the complete comprehension of the Christian message, there must be not only spiritual initiation and illumination but also *spiritual interpretation.* "These things we also speak, not in words which man's wisdom teaches but which the Holy Spirit teaches, comparing spiritual things with spiritual" (v. 13). Now we reach a point in Paul's argument where we need to follow him very closely. These words that we have just quoted are often used as a proof text by the proponents of verbal inspiration, a doctrine that is both biblical and true. But Paul here says "we speak," not "we write." Thus he is referring not so much to inspiration as to interpretation. He is teaching us that the knowledge of truth can be arrived at by an understanding of two necessary essentials.

First, the Spirit's use of language: "These things we also speak, not in words which man's wisdom teaches but which the Holy Spirit teaches" (v. 13). He who knows the mind of God also chooses the words of God to interpret divine truth. This is essentially the ministry of the Holy Spirit. What an importance this places on the Scriptures throughout the church age. His work is to interpret the Bible to men and women who know the experience of spiritual initiation and illumination. Let it be stressed, however, that the Spirit never speaks outside the context of the divine revelation we call the Holy Bible. That is why we need to give special attention to His use of language. Not one jot or tittle is inconsequential. Jesus said, "Heaven and earth will pass away, but My words will by no means pass away" (Matt. 24:35). He added, "When He, the Spirit of truth, has come, He will guide you into all truth" (John 16:13). This is the secret of interpretation: the Spirit using His own words to make known the mind of God.

But with the Spirit's use of language, there is also the Spirit's terms of reference: "The Holy Spirit . . . comparing spiritual things with spiritual" (v. 13). Now commentators have found it difficult to expound this sentence. Some say it means "matching spiritual things with spiritual words." Others maintain that it reads "interpreting spiritual things to spiritual men." I am convinced that both contentions are right. "No prophecy of Scripture is of any private interpretation" (2 Peter 1:20). The Holy Spirit has His terms of reference, and through the body of truth as we know it in the Bible, there is sufficient support for every cardinal doctrine we hold dear.

What is more, we have what is known as a Christian tradition that is made up of the contributions of *spiritual* men down through the centuries. So we are not left to guess about divine revelation. There is no truth that is vital to Christian life and practice that has not the support both of divine revelation and Christian tradition. When Paul writes to Timothy concerning the comprehension and communication of divine truth, he says, "And the things that you have heard from me *among many witnesses,* commit these to faithful men who will be able to teach others also" (2 Tim. 2:2).

So Paul concludes this amazing paragraph by pointing out that "the natural man does not receive the things of the Spirit of God, for they are foolishness to him; nor can he know them, because they are spiritually discerned" (v. 14). In simple language—without spiritual initiation, illumination, and interpretation, divine truth is nothing more than foolishness to the unregenerate—the person of the world. This person looks upon revelation as an absurdity. Once we have understood this we have an explanation of the attitude that is adopted by the non-Christian to spiritual things. We must therefore be patient and pray that he or she may submit to the terms of divine revelation.

On the other hand, says the apostle, "He who is spiritual judges all things, yet he himself is rightly judged by no one" (v. 15). The person who knows spiritual initiation, illumination, and interpretation possesses a faculty that enables him or her to sift and examine things divinely revealed, as well as things human and natural. At the same time, he or she cannot be subject to examination and judgment by the one who is destitute of the Spirit. No unregenerate person has the right to criticize or judge a Christian regarding his or her personal faith in Christ. The unregenerate person is without the faculty of spiritual discernment, and therefore cannot understand the nature of the miracle that has taken place. Just as he or she cannot judge the Christian, so he or she cannot instruct the Lord. It is nothing but human ignorance, if not human impertinence, for the natural man to raise his voice against the God he is unwilling to accept.

By way of contrast, the Christian has the mind of Christ, and this is the transcendent thought with which Paul concludes. The wisdom of God is nothing less than the mind of Christ. The word *mind* here means "intellect" or "consciousness." We have the consciousness of Christ, the mind of Christ, the outlook of Christ. This is not the same word that Paul uses in Philippians 2. There it is the disposition of Christ; here it is the intelligent understanding, or wisdom, of Christ.

How wonderful it is that you and I, by spiritual initiation, illumination, and interpretation, can know the very mind of the Son of God! And the best of it is that throughout time and eternity we are going to continue to explore that mind of Christ, and so become more and more like Jesus. What a vast universe of knowledge, life, and blessing stretches out before us! Even to contemplate it makes us feel like Isaac Newton when he exclaimed, "I am like a little child standing by the seashore, picking up a pebble here and a pebble there, and admiring them while the great sea rolls in front of me."

So Paul climaxes a mighty subject with the loftiest of concepts. What he is saying to these Corinthians is that if they know the initiation, illumination, and interpretation of the Holy Spirit, they will know the mind of Christ. And to know the mind of Christ is to know unity of thought, life, and practice. There is no division in the mind of Christ; therefore, there can be no division in the local church that knows the mind of Christ.

We cannot examine what Paul has to say on this subject of "The Comprehension of the Christian Message" without concluding that there is an inseparable link between the anointing of the Spirit and the mind of Christ. Only as we know this anointing can we communicate the mind of Christ. We may well ask, therefore, how a person can know this anointing of the Spirit. Surely the answer to that question is to turn to the perfect Example, even that of our blessed Lord. His anointing took place on the banks of the Jordan. From His mother's womb He was filled with the Holy Spirit, but the anointing came later at His baptism. As we examine the gospel narrative there appear to be three conditions, or laws, that were fulfilled in order to experience that anointing.

The first was the law of righteousness. Approaching John, Jesus said, "Permit it to be so now, for thus it is fitting for us to fulfill all righteousness" (Matt. 3:15). "Righteousness" is obedience to the revealed will of God in all areas of life. Without this righteousness no one can know the anointing of the Holy Spirit. The Bible says that God gives the Holy Spirit "to those who obey Him" (Acts 5:32). The reason why Christian people do not know the anointing of the Spirit is because they are not prepared to pay the price of obedience in all matters of faith and practice.

But with the law of righteousness there was the law of yieldedness. We read that "[Jesus] . . . had been baptized" (Matt. 3:16). Jesus handed Himself over to John in an act of utter yieldedness. No one can be baptized without submitting himself completely to the baptizer. And it is equally true that no one can be anointed with the Holy Spirit without self-surrender to Jesus as Lord. This is what Paul means when he says, "If you live according to the flesh you will die; but if by the Spirit you put to death the deeds of the body, you will live. For as many as are led by the Spirit of God, these are sons of God" (Rom. 8:13–14). Self-effort has to die if the Holy Spirit is to take over in Lordship and leadership in our lives.

Then there is a third law: it is the law of prayerfulness. Luke tells us that as Jesus "was baptized; and while He *prayed,* the heaven was opened. And the Holy Spirit descended in bodily form like a dove upon Him" (Luke 3:21–22). Now while the Holy Spirit comes to indwell a believer at conversion, the Scriptures make it clear that the anointing of the Spirit is a subsequent and continuous blessing. The anointing I knew yesterday is not sufficient for today. There is no fixation point in the experience of spiritual power. So the Lord Jesus said, "If you then, being evil, know how to give good gifts to your children, how much more will your heavenly Father give the Holy Spirit to those who ask Him!" (Luke 11:13). He also told His disciples to "tarry in the city of Jerusalem until [they were] endued with power from on high" (Luke 24:49). It was while they were praying and waiting on the Lord that they experienced the outpouring of Pentecost.

We need to ask and keep asking if we are to know the anointing of the Spirit. To experience this anointing is to know both the mind and might of Christ in the comprehension and proclamation of the Christian message. The reason why our witness is so ineffective is because we are not prepared to bow to the laws of righteousness, yieldedness, and prayerfulness.

D. L. Moody learned this secret even though, to a certain extent, he was untrained and unlettered. Indeed, he was used like few evangelists in the history of gospel preaching. On one occasion a group of ministers were discussing him in connection with a possible crusade in their city. One young man rose to his feet and said, "Why have we to invite D. L. Moody anyway? Has he a monopoly of the Holy Spirit?" After a pause, a discerning pastor quietly replied, "While Mr. Moody may not have a monopoly of the Holy Spirit, it is very evident that *the Holy Spirit has a monopoly of him.*"

Moody's secret can be yours and mine—*when* we are prepared for the Spirit's monopoly of our lives. Then, and only then, can we know the "anointing from the Holy One" (1 John 2:20); then, and only then, can we appreciate and communicate "The Christian Message for Contemporary Life."

1 Corinthians 3:1-4

I. The Christian Challenge Condemns the Marks of
    Spiritual Babyhood (v. 1)
    A. The Categories of Carnal Christians (2:14–15; 3:1, 3)
        1. There is the Natural Man (2:14)
        2. There is the Spiritual Man (2:15)
        3. There is the Carnal Man (vv. 1, 3)
    B. The Capacity of Carnal Christians (v. 2)
    C. The Conduct of Carnal Christians (vv. 3–4)
        1. Unhealthy Discontent (v. 3)
        2. Unhealthy Discord (v. 3)
        3. Unhealthy Division (vv. 3–4)
II. The Christian Challenge Commends the Marks of
    Spiritual Adulthood (v. 1a)
    A. A Willingness to Accept Spiritual Truth (2:14)
    B. A Willingness to Apply Spiritual Truth (2:13)
    C. A Willingness to Affirm Spiritual Truth (2:15–16)

chapter SIX

THE CHALLENGE
OF THE CHRISTIAN MESSAGE

We have dealt with "The Contradiction of the Christian Message," "The Character of the Christian Message," "The Community of the Christian Message," "The Communication of the Christian Message," and "The Comprehension of the Christian Message." We conclude with "The Challenge of the Christian Message." Paul is still dealing with the matter of comprehension: how to understand the Christian message in order to articulate it with authority. He anticipates the question of how people can know spiritual initiation, illumination, and interpretation and still be infantile in their understanding of the Christian message. The inability to communicate, a problem that faces the Christian church today, can be summed up in one word: "carnality." Because of carnality in the life there is division in the church and confusion in the world, division because we are unsure of our message and confusion because people don't know what to believe. One young lady came to my wife and said, "One section of the church says this, another section of the church says that, and a third group emphasizes some other particular doctrine. Who am I to believe?"

Why is there no clear articulation within the church of

Jesus Christ? The answer to this is twofold: the Christian challenge condemns the marks of spiritual babyhood and, by the same token, the Christian challenge commends the marks of spiritual adulthood.

First of all, *the Christian challenge condemns the marks of spiritual babyhood:* "And I, brethren, could not speak to you as to spiritual people but as to carnal, as to babes in Christ" (v. 1). Paul has the closing verses of the previous chapter in mind. There he spells out the categories of carnal Christians, as well as the capacity of carnal Christians. To get them in perspective, let's look at each of them in detail.

First, there are *the categories of carnal Christians*, chapter 2, verses 14 and 15: "The *natural* man does not receive the things of the Spirit of God, for they are foolishness to him; nor can he know them, because they are spiritually discerned. But he who is *spiritual* judges all things, yet he himself is rightly judged by no one." And in verses 1 and 3 of chapter 3 he adds, "I . . . could not speak to you as to spiritual people but as to *carnal,* as to babes in Christ. . . . For you are still carnal." A glance at those verses reveals that there are three categories of people in any given church.

There is the *natural* man: "The *natural* man does not receive the things of the Spirit of God, for they are foolishness to him; nor can he know them, because they are spiritually discerned." Chapter 2, verse 14, tells us that "the natural man," the unregenerate man, is the person who is born in sin (Ps. 51:5). Yes, he may be educated and refined, but he is still unregenerate; he is still destitute of that divine content imparted by the regenerating power of the Holy Spirit. There are many men and women in our churches or in the world today who appeal to us in every respect; yet to know them is to discover that they are lost and undone, because they are still "dead in trespasses and sins" (Eph. 2:1). They attend church, but arc not part of the true church.

There is the *spiritual* man: "He who is *spiritual* judges all things, yet he himself is rightly judged by no one" (1 Cor. 2:15). The spiritual man, of course, is the person who knows what it is to be born again. He has two births, the natural birth and the spiritual birth. The first came through Adam; the second, through the last Adam, even our Lord Jesus Christ. Since the nature of the spiritual person is spiritual, the development is totally and always spiritual.

Suffice it to say that the most important thing in the spiritual life is development and growth. It is dangerously possible to reach what the psychologists call the fixation point in our physical, mental, emotional, and spiritual development. We have undoubtedly met people who don't seem to grow; their spiritual life is static and stunted. They still talk about their initial conversion or some great mountain-peak experience, but it is all in the past. There is nothing new, nothing relevant and fresh. It is all backdated and stale. We might well ask: Can we produce growth? The answer, of course, is No. The power to grow spiritually is within the nature of the divine life within us. God alone causes us to grow and develop.

It is likewise true that there are certain conditions that encourage growth. We are exhorted by Peter to "grow in the grace and knowledge of our Lord and Savior Jesus Christ" (2 Peter 3:18). Very simply, it entails abiding in the grace and truth revealed in our Lord Jesus Christ. Grace is the fullness of the Holy Spirit in us day by day (Eph. 5:18); truth is the Word of God dwelling in us richly and deeply (Col. 3:16). This calls for surrendering the frontiers of our spiritual capacities so that we might receive more grace through the Holy Spirit in order that we might go on to greater heights of truth and obedience.

There is the *carnal* man: "I, brethren, could not speak to you as to spiritual people but as to carnal *(sarkinos),* as to babes in Christ" (v. 1). Significantly, in verse 3 Paul adds, "You are still carnal." To understand the characteristics of a carnal Christian, Paul differentiates between two words that are translated in our Authorized Version as "carnal," but are quite different in the Greek. In the first instance, the word *carnal,* in verse 1, "signifies the partaking of the nature of the flesh." But in the other reference the apostle uses a more severe term *(sarkikos),* which means *sensual* and implies a life "under the control of a fleshly nature."[1] W. E. Vine affirms this in the first usage of the term *carnal:* In verse 1 the Corinthians were not showing progress because they were babes. In respect of the term used in verse 3, however, their jealousy and strife rendered them guilty of yielding to the lusts that had their source in man's corrupt and fallen nature. So, as babes, it is possible to be carnal in the sense that we are living under the domination of that fallen and corrupt nature, despite the striving of the Spirit within us, with the result that our spiritual life is dwarfed and our spiritual walk is defeated.

What category are you in, my friend? The natural? The spiritual? Or the carnal? If you are characterized by the natural man, then you are not born again because you have never repented at the foot of the cross or received the gift of God's salvation in Christ. If you are spiritual, then you know that quiet sense of divine assurance and adequacy; your life is filled with the Holy Spirit. If you are carnal, then you are still under the control of your fleshly, corrupt nature. But with those categories of carnal Christians, notice the capacity of carnal Christians: "I fed you with milk and not with solid food; for until now you were not able to receive it, and even now you are still not able" (v. 2). The capacity of carnal Christians is pathetically limited, for it is restricted to a baby's formula of milk. The apostle longed to feed the Corinthians on the meat of the Word, but he could not; they couldn't take it. As the writer to the Hebrews points out, "Solid food belongs to those who are of full age, that is, those who by reason of use have their senses exercised to discern both good and evil" (Heb. 5:14). Meat is for those who are spiritual. But for those who never measure up to the challenge of maturity, there is carnality; they are incapable of appreciating the meat of the Word: "And I, brethren, could not speak to you as to spiritual people but as to carnal, as to babes in Christ" (v. 1). Although the apostle uses the affectionate term *brethren,* he is actually rebuking them for failure to appreciate "the deep things of God" (1 Cor. 2:9–10).

Nothing is more disappointing and discouraging to a preacher of the gospel than to minister to a congregation of infants who never grow up spiritually. How true this is of so many Christians throughout the church today! They have been saved for years, but they are still drinking milk; they are still wrapped up in the baby garments of their first days in Christ. Through a lack of growth they are incapable of appreciating the meat of the Word.

But even more serious, they are incapable of *appropriating* the meat of the Word: "I fed you with milk and not with solid food; for until now you were not able to receive it" (v. 2). So many individuals who attend church go out from the service absolutely bored, without having appropriated what God had for them. Such carnal people, according to Hebrews 5:13, are "unskilled in the word of righteousness." "The word of righteousness" signifies the fully developed Christian teaching. Therefore, by "unskilled in the word of righteousness," the writer refers to the inexperience of Christians in following the exegesis and exposition of divine truth. While they sit at God's banquet table, they fail to order from God's 66-book menu! Paul admonished his son in the faith, "Be diligent to present yourself approved to God, a worker who does not need to be ashamed, rightly dividing the word of truth" (2 Tim. 2:15).

Do *you* fail in your appreciation and appropriation of divine truth? After years of so-called church life, are you still inexperienced and unskillful in the word of righteousness? If so, you give evidence of being an infant and, therefore, carnal.

Have you ever visited a home for people who are mentally slow? It is one of the most heartbreaking experiences a person can have. I recall one individual I used to see in a home in England. The features and proportions were those of a person about thirty years of age, yet that dear fellow had the mentality and behavior of a little boy. Time and again I said to myself, "If this is the kind of effect that this person has on my heart, what must God feel like when He looks upon a congregation of carnal Christians who have never grown up spiritually?"

But now let's look at the conduct of carnal Christians: "For you are still carnal. For where there are envy, strife, and divisions among you, are you not carnal and behaving like mere men? For when one says, 'I am of Paul,' and another, 'I am of Apollos,' are you not carnal?" (vv. 3–4). In this classic word picture of spiritual babyhood, Paul tells us that the believer who never seems to move past the childish stage is carnal in his behavior. Such people are characterized by three things: first of all, unhealthy discontent: "There [is] . . . envy" (v. 3). The word *envy* in the Greek means zeal out of control, which easily leads to jealousy and the like. How accurate Paul is! Some children are discontented and envious when they cease to be the center of attraction. In a similar way, these Corinthian "babies" focused more on personalities and name-dropping than on preaching. What really mattered was whether they belonged to the prominent section of the church. God preserve us from such carnality and fleshly lust!

But unhealthy discontent leads to unhealthy discord:

"There [is] . . . strife" (v. 3). That word *strife* denotes wrangling, or what *Phillips* renders as "squabbling." With a nursery of discontented babies it will not be long before there is discord and strife. The same is true of the church. Where there are those who refuse to grow up, there is always wrangling and squabbling. Everything that happens and everyone who ministers becomes a bone of contention.

Such discontent and discord leads to unhealthy division: "There [are] divisions among you. . . . For . . . one says, 'I am of Paul,' and another, 'I am of Apollos'" (vv. 3–4). And he asks, "Are you not carnal?" (v. 4). Though the word *divisions* is not in the best manuscripts, the thought is clear here. Paul speaks of the factions and cliques that these carnal Christians had created in Corinth. Instead of finding their center in Christ, they were saying "I am of Paul," . . . "I am of Apollos," . . . "I am of Cephas," . . . "I am of Christ" (1 Cor. 1:12). They were guilty of bringing Christ down to the level of men, comparing Him with Apollos, Cephas, and Paul. Jesus is not to be compared with anyone. He is unique. He is singular. He is supreme. He is preeminent. These people had lost that majestic concept. Why? Because they were infantile and immature. Whether in Paul's day or our day, the sure evidence of such thinking is babyhood.

Are you characterized by these marks of carnality? Do you create discontent, discord, and division? How repelling are these traits of the uncrucified flesh and yet how often they are seen in our lives! The challenge of the Christian message condemns the marks of spiritual babyhood because these are the very things that stifle the articulation of the gospel to the outside world. The world will not believe until they see a unified and purified church that proclaims an authoritative message of the gospel. As we examine ourselves in the light of this exposition, how it makes us want to grow up until we have left spiritual babyhood behind. No wonder

Paul could write in this same epistle, "When I was a child, I spoke as a child, I understood as a child, I thought as a child; but when I became a man, I put away childish things" (1 Cor. 13:11).

While the Christian challenge condemns the marks of spiritual babyhood, *the Christian challenge commends the marks of spiritual adulthood:* "And I, brethren, could not speak to you as to spiritual people" (v. 1). While babyhood has the mark of carnality, adulthood has the mark of maturity, and it is all wrapped up in that little word *spiritual* that Paul uses repeatedly.

Glance back to the previous chapter, where we find three aspects of this maturity. In verse 13 onward, Paul says:

> These things we also speak, not in words which man's wisdom teaches but which the Holy Spirit teaches, comparing spiritual things with spiritual. But the natural man does not receive the things of the Spirit of God, for they are foolishness to him; nor can he know them, because they are spiritually discerned. . . . He who is spiritual judges all things, yet he himself is rightly judged by no one. (vv. 13–15)

Then he picks up that word *spiritual* in the opening verse of chapter 3: He wishes he could speak to them as spiritual people.

One of the marks of maturity is a willingness to *accept* spiritual truth. In verse 14 of chapter 2 we read, "But the natural man does not receive [literally "accepts not"] the things of the Spirit of God," implying that the spiritual man does so because such things are spiritually discerned. The acid test of maturity in one's life is a willingness to accept spiritual truth. It means you have a discernment for truth: you seek the church, you seek out the minister, you seek a Bible teacher who has an evident anointing of the Spirit upon his life. Whatever the cost, you desire spiritual truth. Paul says, "All Scripture is given by inspiration of God, and is profitable for doctrine, for reproof, for correction, for instruction in righteousness, that the man of God may be complete, thoroughly equipped [rounded out, mature, equipped] for every good work" (2 Tim. 3:16–17).

The test of spiritual maturity is that wherever spiritual truth is found—whether it comes in the form of doctrine, or reproof, or correction, or instruction in righteousness—you are there under the sentence and authority of God's Word. As I travel, I am delighted to discover that more and more young people are willing to listen to revealed truth and hunger for more.

Second, there must be a willingness to *apply* spiritual truth: "These things we also speak, not in words that man's wisdom teaches but which the Holy Spirit teaches, *comparing spiritual things with spiritual*" (1 Cor. 2:13). Scholars have wrangled over those words throughout the centuries, but the Authorized Version is as accurate as any of the alternative renderings. Paul is saying that God the Holy Spirit speaks to us, bringing spiritual words to those who are prepared to accept and apply them. We can absorb truth Sunday after Sunday until we are like saturated sponges, but it is only when we apply the truth that something begins to happen.

Some years ago I was preaching at a convention in Barbados, the West Indies. Sharing the ministry with me was an Anglican clergyman by the name of the Reverend Ian Barclay. At the time he was the Associate Rector of St. Helen's Church in London, located near the Stock Exchange, where every week they hosted eight hundred to nine hundred businessmen for lunch-hour services.

Later he became vicar of his own church with curates under him. Often in the Anglican church, curates share the ministry, with the vicar reading the lesson and the curate preaching. After reading the lesson Ian Barclay would step down from the pulpit and sit in the front row and listen to his curate preach.

He told me that one day, his wardens came to criticize him. "How can you ever do such a thing?" they wanted to know. "You are the vicar of this church. How can you sit under your curate?" His reply was: "Men, your criticism is a sign of immaturity. It isn't the curate that I am listening to, it is God. I want to sit under the judgment of the Word. Whatever my curate has to say is the voice of God with a message to my heart, and I have to apply it."

One of the greatest sins of the evangelical church is that we have the truth, we have our outlines, we have our notebooks full of information, but we don't apply the truth; we don't sit under the sentence of the Word. We don't let the sermon become experiential in terms of behavior patterns.

The marks of a spiritual person, then, are a willingness to accept the truth; secondly, a willingness to apply the truth; and then, thirdly—and most importantly—a willingness to *affirm* the truth: "He who is spiritual judges all things, yet he himself is rightly judged by no one. For 'who has known the mind of the Lord that he may instruct him?' But we have the mind of Christ" (1 Cor. 2:15–16). The phrase *judges all things* means that as the believer goes out to assess situations in the context of the church, the home, and the world, he or she is affirming the truth as it impinges on the issues of contemporary life, irrespective of what people will say by way of criticism. The text goes on to state, "He who is spiritual judges all things, yet he himself is rightly judged by no one" (v. 15). The language of his or her heart is: "Let the critical darts strike where they may, I am affirming what God has said to me. If I have the mind of Christ, and I am convinced that the Holy Spirit has authenticated the truth in my heart by the Word of God, it matters not who censures or criticizes. I affirm the truth."

This, then, is the challenge of the Christian message, as we face the world with the glorious gospel. What invalidates our gospel testimony is carnality. The Christian message condemns all marks of *carnality*. On the other hand, what authenticates our gospel testimony is *maturity*—a willingness to accept, apply, and affirm spiritual truth unashamedly, cost what it will, because we have the mind of Christ.

Alexander the Great was one of the mightiest conquerors of all time. When he died of a fever at the age of thirty-three, he had conquered the then-known world. History records that on one occasion, while he was sitting in judgment on a number of state matters, a young soldier was brought before him, charged with being a deserter. Alexander was a general who demanded total and complete allegiance; yet here was a deserter. What was he to do with him? He questioned him and the young soldier pleaded guilty and asked for clemency. Surrounded by his aides, the face of the great general slowly relaxed and they heaved a sigh of relief. Would the culprit be released? There was a pause. Then Alexander bent forward and addressed the young man, "What is your name?" Back came a feeble reply, "Alexander." "What is your name?" demanded the Macedonian monarch. The young man said politely, "Alexander, sir." Rising to his feet, the king grabbed the soldier and knocked him to the ground, pinning him to the floor and thundered, "Either change your name or change your behavior."

Unseen to natural eye, but real to faith, our precious Lord stands in our midst and issues a similar challenge: "Either change your name or change your behavior." Repudiate carnality and appropriate maturity. Enter into the fullness of what God can do in you and through you in order that the world may believe. God is looking for individuals in the home, in the workplace, and on the college campus who can speak with an authority that is irresistible. He wants

Christians who accept the truth, apply the truth, and affirm the truth with a sagacity that cannot be repudiated or denied. May the Holy Spirit enable all of us to face and fulfill the challenge of the Christian message so that the world may believe that God has sent His Son to be the Savior of the world; for His Name's sake—amen!

ENDNOTES

Preface

1. Michael Green, *Man Alive* (London: InterVarsity, 1967), preface.

Chapter One

1. William Barclay, *The Letters to the Corinthians* (Edinburgh: Saint Andrew Press, 1958), 16.

Chapter Two

1. James Packer, *God Hath Spoken* (London: Hodder & Stoughton, 1965), 9.
2. Gene Edward Veith, "Catechesis, Preaching, Vocation," in *Here We Stand: A Call from Confessing Evangelicals,* ed. James Montgomery Boice and Benjamin E. Sasse (Grand Rapids: Baker, 1996), 78–79.
3. Leon Morris, *1 Corinthians* (London: Tyndale, 1958), 45.

Chapter Three

1. G. Campbell Morgan, *The Corinthian Letters of Paul* (London: Charles Higham and Son, 1947), 28.

Chapter Four

1. Bishop Lightfoot.
2. Leon Morris, *1 Corinthians* (London: Tyndale, 1958), 52.

Chapter Five

1. G. Campbell Morgan, 33.
2. William Barclay, 29.
3. Herschel H. Hobbs, *The Epistles to the Corinthians* (Grand Rapids: Baker, 1960), 23.

Chapter Six

1. W. E. Vine, *First Corinthians* (London: Oliphants, 1951), 44–45.

P.O. Box 757800, Memphis, TN 38175-7800 • (901) 757-7977
Fax: (901) 757-1372 • www.olford.org • Olford@ixlmemphis.com

OUR HISTORY

The Stephen Olford Center for Biblical Preaching was dedicated on June 4, 1988, in Memphis, Tennessee. It is the international headquarters for Encounter Ministries, Inc., and houses the Institute for Biblical Preaching.

The Institute for Biblical Preaching was founded in 1980 to promote biblical preaching and practical training for pastors, evangelists, and lay leaders. After fifty years of pastoral and global ministry, Dr. Olford believes that the ultimate answer to the problems of every age is the anointed expository preaching of God's inerrant Word. Such preaching must be restored to the contemporary pulpit!

OUR STRATEGY

The purpose of the Institute for Biblical Preaching is to equip and encourage pastors and laymen in expository preaching and exemplary living, to the end that the church will be revived and the world will be reached with the saving Word of Christ. The program includes:

- *Institutes* and special events on expository preaching, pastoral leadership, essentials of evangelism, the fullness of the Holy Spirit, the reality of revival, and other related subjects.

- *Workshops* for pastors and laymen to preach "live" in order to have their sermons, skills, and styles critiqued constructively.

- *1-Day Video Institutes* on Anointed Biblical Preaching hosted around the country for pastors and laymen who invite us.

- *Consultations* on pastoral and practical matters.

- *Outreach* through wider preaching/teaching ministry, radio broadcasting, literature, audio/video resources, and web site.